The PSYCHIC Workshop

A Complete Program for Fulfilling Your Spiritual Potential

KIM CHESTNEY

Adams Media
Avon, Massachusetts

Published by
Adams Media, an F+W Publications Company
57 Littlefield Street, Avon, MA 02322. U.S.A.
www.adamsmedia.com

ISBN: 1-59337-021-0

Printed in Canada.

J I H G F E D C B A

Library of Congress Cataloging-in-Publication Data
Chestney, Kim.
The psychic workshop / Kim Chestney.
p. cm.
ISBN 1-59337-021-0
1. Psychic ability. I. Title.
BF1031.C49 2004
133.8—dc22
2003028016

Cover illustration by © Vicky Emptage / Getty Images.

For Barbara,
who showed me that
all I ever wanted to see
was not invisible to me

epiphany

june afternoon sunshine and breeze fleeting soon, all gold, and me with my blue blanket, cat sleeping, willow weeping out back to back lilacs on the wind, winding in and out of these white rooms, my wandering mind, in another time, discovering a long-lost place, in a hint of time, a trace of space . . .

. . . wild ocean and me in between the walking dunes, their desolate tunes and sea spray songs, I think I'd like to sing along, along the sunset—with a ghostly silhouette, and the sky forever on this empty beach full of whispers, full of mystery, and tempting fears; should I leave and sow my tears, or walk on, walk on with You at my side, with my heart as your bride, I'd sense the spirit of this land, in the softness of the sinking sands and easy bliss, the world itself seems all amiss; we'd all exist, with no care—for who, or when or where—or wasted lives and nine to fives, trifling, stifling, promises, bribes—play your tune on our deaf ears, upon this rapture, we lay our fears . . .

. . . until this world, it fades, shades down, and wide awake—above, inside, beneath the skies the shrine of the stars, the pull of the tides; behind these—eyes every place, every passion in sensory fashion for an instant, forever—for every, every everything: all I know, all I do, all is Love, all is You . . . and I am left, right back safe in my skin, the truth within, with more than money can ever buy—the real discovery that lives in seeing with new eyes.

—*KC*
Cape Henelopen, Delaware

Contents

Acknowledgments

It has been said that when the student is ready, the teacher appears. The making of this book is greatly due to the wisdom of many treasured teachers and friends, all of whom seemed to arrive just when they were most needed. To those who have guided and inspired me—Rebecca Troup, Rev. Wendy Goodman, and Rev. Peggy Elkus. To those who have encouraged me and shared in the journey—Clyde, Joetta, and, especially, to JoAnn—who made a believer of me.

A special thank-you to Jeff Herman and Danielle Chiotti for believing in this project, and helping to make the idea into a reality. Thanks also to all of my friends and family members who have stood by me on the road less traveled, who have been my light in dark places—to the kindred spirits who travel life with me. You know who you are.

INTRODUCTION

BEYOND SAINTS AND PSYCHICS

You have never talked to a mere mortal.

—C. S. Lewis, The Weight of Glory

There are no ordinary people. The blur of everyday reality has created a world in which most of us have forgotten the value of our unique and sacred existence. We all are human. We all die. But, more important, we all are more than human, and we all live on. We are more than laborers and artists, parents and children, masters and servants; our earthly occupations are the expressions of the unfathomable energy that exists as our true selves. It is this true self, once rediscovered, that enables us to understand more clearly the nature of our world, and our own existence.

With this awareness, everyday experiences become mystical experiences of their own. The profound beauty that stirs our soul during a summer sunset; the smile of a child, or friend, or lover that warms our heart; the quiet way the light glows through a window on a cold, snowy evening; all of these are simple ways we experience the beauty of creation. But not all expression of the higher powers is so subtle. There are moments when the veil between our world and the heavens is pulled wide open. The laws of physics are violated. We imagine the unimaginable, experience the impossible. These moments have been the foundation of most of the religions we know in human history. These are the moments of revelation.

The saints, the seers, the psychics, the shamans, the prophets, the oracles, the mystics, the yogis, the diviners, the high priests and priestesses—they have had many names throughout history—they are the ones who have dedicated their lives to the understanding and experience of these mysteries. But where are they today? Who are the prophets among us now? Who, in our own day and age, hears the voice of God?

Most of us have lived our lives with the notion that heavenly experience is reserved for the select few—for the saints, for the blessed ones. We may be moved by the raptures of St. Theresa, or inspired by St. Thomas Aquinas's mysticism, but few consider such destinies attainable. We think that there must be something innately *different* about such people, something special that allows them to understand God in ways that we cannot. But, in truth, the heavenly powers reveal to us all. We are all blessed ones. Heaven is no longer in the clouds. It is right here, all around us, everywhere; we must only open our eyes to see it.

We are all completely capable of transcending our mundane existence to reach an awareness of a higher reality. We simply aren't aware of our own potential. We even limit ourselves under the false assumption that psychics, like the saints, are somehow *different* from us, that they were born with a special ability that we lack. This is not the case. Though these individuals may have natural talents, or callings, that are stronger than ours, the potential for each of us is always there.

Intuitive ability is a skill, a talent to be developed like any other. Do we assume that, because we weren't born with the ability to play the piano, we will never be able to do it? Do we give up ... because we weren't born with an innate understa... do not. We become experts with ti... We may have been born with a ... that doesn't mean we don't have t... composition, or line weight, just li... mean that less creative individuals ... r own dedication, successful artis...

... t, spiritual or intuitive or "psychi... ose to call them—are uniquely de... We just need to take the time to di... be saints *or* psychics for Heaven t... open our hearts and minds to the i... e just beyond our five senses.

... rld lies in cultivating our intuition ... voice of quiet knowing. It is a voice that is so g... that we often cannot distinguish it from our own thoughts. Whether or not we are aware of it, our intuition guides us every day. It is more than perceptiveness, more than a conscience—it is the meeting point of our conscious mind and the spiritual realm. This "intuitive point" is where we receive impressions from the higher realms, as we are nudged with intuitive feelings. The more we pay attention to our intuition, the easier it becomes to build a conscious rapport with our heavenly guidance.

When we feel connected with the metaphysical world, we experience, firsthand, the continuous structure of life—a life that does not end with the death of our physical bodies. We remind ourselves that there is no end to love, both the love we have for our friends in this world and love God has for us. We live more balanced and fulfilled lives, living as a part of the peaceful, creative Spirit that unites us all. We develop our selves for the good of humanity, as well as for our own evolution. By raising our own awareness, we are taking one small step to raise the awareness of our world. With a true understanding of the higher powers, we live better and more genuine lives. By living in tandem with the spirit world, we can share the beauty of life with our brothers and sisters both in this world and beyond.

Part One

Awakening the Spirit: *Understanding the Meaningful Nature of Life*

One's own unconquered soul is one's greatest enemy.

—*Excerpt from a Jain prayer*

The most beautiful experience we can have is the mysterious—the fundamental emotion which stands at the cradle of true art and true science.

—*Einstein,* Living Philosophies, *1931*

CHAPTER 1

BUILD YOUR MYSTERY: *The Perfection of Souls*

The soul itself is the center of all that we have come to call "psychic." The word itself translates literally to mean "of the soul." When we embrace our psychic potential, we embrace our soul's potential—the potential to use our innate ability to connect with the natural forces that lie beyond the material world, beyond the five senses. By calling ourselves psychic, or even intuitive, we are, essentially, referring to our soul's heightened state of sensitivity or perceptivity to the extraordinary mysteries of life itself.

The longer we make the everyday world our home, the easier it becomes to forget about our spiritual home. As children, we found mystery, magic, and adventure everywhere, in the simplest of things. Our backyards were full of secret gardens, castles, and forts; we were heroes, heroines, magicians, and adventurers, even if only in our imagination. The whole, huge world was an open book, an unknown land to be sought, discovered, and conquered. Life was ensconced in mystery; nothing was yet so familiar that we would tire of it.

Today, we find ourselves in a place where all of the lands are mapped and all of the waters are charted. Everything makes sense; everything is explained, categorized, and put into its place. Our world suddenly seems a lot smaller, and a lot less interesting. But that's *reality*. Or is it?

Is there more to life than this? Does not a part of us long to rekindle that spirit of adventure in our heart? Has the drag of routine and reality left our senses dull? How has the vibrant adventure of childhood morphed into the rational repetition that so many of us call adulthood? Where has the mystery gone?

The answer is that the mystery hasn't gone anywhere; we have. Time takes us to a place of sobriety where childhood whimsy withers in neglect. There comes a point in life when we become too self-conscious to play, or to pretend; when reality asserts its dominance over imagination, making us strong and smart, and, ideally, socially adjusted. But, as time passes, we begin to notice a little something tugging at us—maybe a desire to create something, or to play a musical instrument, or to build new things, or to fall in love again—something that keeps us from settling too long into the wake-wash-and-work routine. Something that keeps us feeling *alive.*

Imagine all that we can do, if we set our hearts to it. Not one thing has been accomplished that has not yet first been imagined. A fertile imagination is a garden in which we sow the seeds of every accomplishment, including the development of our intuition. To free our intuition, we must first free our minds of the limitations that prevent true expression. We must, in the simplest of terms, open our minds to unknown possibility, release our judgments and expectations, and come full circle. We must return to our youthful hearts with the wisdom of our years intact. We must become wise children.

It is no surprise that children are often quite open to the spiritual realm. Not only are they chronologically closer to it, in terms of linear time, but they have not been here long enough to let this world condition them to the perimeters of reality. They see while we are blind and they hear while we are deaf, because their minds are young, free, and open. If we want to see, if we want to believe, we must resurrect that childlike imagination. Create. Play. Imagine the possibilities. Be inspired.

If we free our lives from the excess clutter of work, anxiety, and stress, our intuition will regenerate. Our minds will be clearer. Our hearts will be calmer. However, if we continue on the "adult" path with our worldly fears and motivations unchecked, *the creeping death* (this is a reference to a term used by C. S. Lewis in his writings) will consume us with lives of terminal insatiability. How easily we lose track of our souls when we remain in perpetual pursuit of the perfect life, the perfect person, the perfect fix. When we look outside ourselves for our inner fulfillment, something will always be missing—there will always be something new to buy, a more challenging job to be had, a more interesting person to fall in love with; but when we look within, we will understand that we have all that we truly need. If we avoid introspection, inevitably, the moment will arrive when our bluff is called, when we have no choice but to burn down the house. Whether this moment comes as a tragedy or as a dream come true, it is a moment when we have the opportunity to replace our illusions with our imagination, our limitations with possibilities, our fears with faith, and our stress with self-expression. It is a moment when life is restored and we are freed.

After that moment, we can begin to live in true harmony with our higher selves and our intuition. Our intuition will always guide us down the path that leads most directly to Heaven. It is not confined by social mores or the status quo, nor is it bound by dogma or earthly tradition. The Eternal One is concerned about nothing more than making our souls perfect.

Tis the witching hour of night,
Orbed is the moon and bright,
And the stars they glisten, glisten,
Seeming with bright eyes to listen
For what listen they?

—John Keats (1795–1821)

CHAPTER 2

THE SOUND OF SILENCE: *Hearing Heaven's Word*

As children, most of us were taught to say our prayers before bed, to give thanks for all that we have, and ask God for the rest that we want. We get so busy with our lives, always asking and wanting and wishing and doing, that God's voice wouldn't have a prayer against the din of our thoughts. But the lines to Heaven run both ways. We can talk, and we can listen. The heavens may not speak to us in a booming voice from the clouds, or in a burning bush—but then again, they may. The miraculous happens when we look beyond ourselves.

God can speak loud and clear when the necessity arises. Near-death experiences have transformed many lives. Countless people will attest to being helped by angels, or to having had premonitions, visions, or extraordinary dreams. But what about those to whom God remains silent? The irony is that God is not ever really silent, we just can't hear. Heaven is always with us, whispering in our ears . . . a call, waiting to be heeded.

To listen, we must quiet our minds. Never will we be listeners while we are caught up in our own desires and self-expression. By releasing our attachments and expectations, and opening our selves to what Heaven has to offer, instead of what we think we want, we open the lines of communication.

Meditation is the first step in building a consciously communicative relationship with the spiritual world. Meditation is not about quieting your mind to the point of vacant boredom or sleep. It is about quieting your mind in order to fill it with other things—heavenly things, better things than worries and petty thoughts. Meditation can be extremely interesting. It is where we meet our higher selves, where we release ourselves from the grip of our daily burdens, where we raise our consciousness, where we receive answers and guidance, where we may interact with spiritual beings on a conscious level.

So, what exactly is our "higher self"? To begin with, a higher self implies the existence of a lower self. If we see our "self" as a consciousness that vacillates between higher and lower levels of awareness, we will understand that when we embrace our higher self, we intend to make ourselves more than we are, better than we are; when we live in our lower self, we wrap ourselves up in our ego personalities, where it is easy to become trapped by our desires and subjective points of view. Our egos are, ultimately, illusions of our own perspective. Our higher self is a point of awareness that transcends our ego drives. To live from our higher self is to live in a state of deeper awareness, which is a vital part of spiritual evolution and self-realization.

Our intuition is our primary link to our higher self, and the higher states of consciousness that accompany it. Our higher self speaks to us through our intuition. But how do we know the divine voice when we hear it? How do we know the answers to our questions? How do we know that our experiences are not tricks of our imagination? The answers to all of these questions come with a deeper understanding and reliance on our intuition. To understand our intuition fully, we should recognize the following:

- There exists a universal creative energy that unites all living things.
- Death is not an end, but a transition that takes us to another realm of existence.

Most spiritual belief systems are based on the notion of humankind's self-mastery. We are here on this earth to evolve, not just as physical beings but as spiritual beings. We learn from our mistakes. Whether we are following the Eightfold Path to Enlightenment or avoiding the Seven Deadly Sins, life is a course that allows us to master our weakness and triumph over our selves. The spirit of God is within all living beings and is all around us, bringing opportunity and inspiring us to make the right choices.

And that is the reason for our lives: To better ourselves, to grow closer to God, and to become perfect. The closer we are to God, the more we are fulfilled, the more we are complete. Each day that we open our hearts to love, beauty, play, friendship, laughter, joy, hope, or tenderness, we live more in the heavenly spirit that calls each of us back to the only home for which we were made.

Time is the substance from which I am made.
Time is a river which carries me along, but I am the river;
it is a tiger that devours me, but I am the tiger;
it is a fire that consumes me, but I am the fire.

—*Jorge Luis Borges*

CHAPTER 3

CIRCLE OF LIFE: *Karma and Spiritual Evolution*

If we are attempting to return to a place, it is only natural to assume that, for one reason or another, we left that place. There was a time when we bade farewell to our heavenly homes and began our descent to the physical plane, to start new lives here. We gave up a state of grace to experience a state of conflict, one that is essential for soul growth. Perhaps the reason for this "fall" cannot be fully comprehended at our level of awareness, but there is little doubt that we are all living in a world of chaos—a world of the most selfless good, as well as the most unspeakable evil; a place where profound beauty and love exist alongside unfathomable suffering and torment. We live day to day, triumph to tragedy.

The tragedy part often makes people doubt the existence of God. How could God allow so much suffering? How could God hurt people this way? But we know better. We understand that God does not create suffering; man creates his own suffering. Human beings create anguish when they deny their inner truths. Surely, God wants nothing more than for us to live lives of peace, but at this stage in the game, we do not always choose peace. Nor should we. It is often our most difficult trials and tribulations that bring us the greatest good.

There is nothing like a good challenge to build character, but whatever we choose, we must choose in the spirit of self-awareness and change for the better. Success is a good thing, but success at the price of the love of our family is not. Money is a good thing, but money at the price of our integrity is not. Misplaced desires, fears, and selfishness have driven us all to hurt others at some point in our lives, and when we hurt others, the worst damage comes to ourselves.

Hence, the wheel of karma begins to turn. The concept of karma reflects the universal law of cause and effect: What comes around goes around; what you sow, you reap; or, as Sir Isaac Newton put it, for every action there is an equal and opposite reaction. Karma is the means of universal balance. When our actions create an imbalance, we must, at some point in time, rebalance that energy. When we cease to create imbalance, we cease to be bound by karmic forces that stand between us and eternal harmony.

The source of karmic imbalance is desire:

> *The karmic law requires that every human wish find ultimate fulfillment. Non-spiritual desires are thus the chain that binds man to the wheel of reincarnation.*
>
> —*Paramahansa Yogananda*

When we desire things or situations in our lives that diminish our spiritual level, we immerse ourselves in the karmic cycle. This cycle connects to the core of our souls, and goes beyond physical life and death.

Two-thirds of the world's people believe in reincarnation—the notion that our souls return to earth for successive lifetimes of spiritual growth and evolution. Karma, along with many of our life circumstances and personal relationships, carries over from life to life, until we release our attachments to the desires that fuel the karmic cycle. Any misplaced attachments to the physical realm create suffering and prevent enlightenment. As we begin to realize that our real treasures lay beyond the transient material world, we take the first steps in liberating our souls from this process.

Seen through the perspective of karma, our world suddenly does not seem so tragic after all. Every experience is, inevitably, an experience in growth, balance, and justice. Crime and punishment become the most personal of experiences. For example, say that a perpetrator harms a victim. Until we understand karma, we will realize that the perpetrator is the cause of the harmful action, but we fail to realize that the victim also attracted the perpetrator. On a deeper level, each sought out the other in order to learn a lesson, to restore balance, or to neutralize a destructive desire that (often unconsciously) bound the two to begin with.

It is also possible to release our selves from our karmic ties by raising our awareness. We find our true release when we relinquish our attachments and give up our will to the divine way. We will always have free will: the will to choose to learn through karma (the hard way) or to learn through awareness and release. The wheel must stop somewhere.

When we begin to connect with our higher selves, we rise above our egos and we rise above the karmic cycle. We no longer desire revenge on those who have wronged us; we no longer wrong others by means of our distorted desires. We choose instead to desire the one thing that will never diminish us: to live in the loving spirit of creation. When our wordly desires are put into this perspective, everything else will naturally fall into its place. When we embrace our inner divinity, we fulfill ourselves; when we fulfill ourselves, we are able to help fulfill others with our love and support.

Our doubts are traitors,
And make us lose the good we oft might win
By fearing to attempt.

—William Shakespeare

CHAPTER 4

FEARLESSNESS: *Finding Freedom Through Faith*

It has been said that the opposite of love is hate, though some say that its real opposite is apathy. But when it comes to matters of the soul, what stands in true opposition to love is fear. There is a lot of truth in the old saying: There is nothing to fear but fear itself. Fear undermines our aspirations and our pleasures, our trust and our relationships. When we allow ourselves to be afraid as we travel down life's path, we are forgetting that we are always in Heaven's hands. We are all on this roller coaster of life; we can hang on and enjoy the ride, or we can ride it out in anguish, afraid and holding on for our lives. The end is the same, either way. We finish the ride.

But how are we to be fearless in such a dangerous world? The wheel of karma has spun us all into lives that are never *safe* from suffering. But life isn't about being safe. We will never experience our full potential while we are operating under the policy of safety first. The chances we take, the compromises that we avoid, are the actions that keep our souls alive. And it is our times of suffering that bring our greatest growth.

The same concepts apply to intuitive development. Our fears are our biggest deterrents. Among those fears are tragic misconceptions regarding the nature of the spiritual realm. We have all heard the horror stories, the accounts of malevolent, invisible beings ravishing helpless innocents. We've all seen *The Exorcist.* Possessions, ghosts, devils, poltergeists, and the like feed our fears and make us reluctant to delve into the spiritual world at all. Hollywood and horror films perpetuate the myths of evil that cause many of us to shy away from our spirituality.

We all have our dark sides. We all have at least one inner "demon" to fight jealousy, greed, pride. When we conquer our vices and human weaknesses, we release a negative energy that we have been carrying with us, even subconsciously. This release liberates our souls and raises us to a new spirit level. The old things that once troubled us no longer faze us; what once had power over us is now at our mercy. We will notice that the negativity or disruption in our lives gradually begins to fade away. The darkness no longer has a hold on us.

This process applies to us internally as well as externally. In the spirit world, the more evolved souls will be attracted to the higher vibrational energies within us, including love, hope, and joy; less evolved souls may align themselves with our lower vibrational energies, such as anger, resentment, or treachery. We can liken this process to human social interaction. For example, when we go to a party, we walk into a room where we meet all kinds of people. Some are like us, and some are not like us at all. We will be attracted to some, repulsed by others. It is the same with our friends on the other side; they are attracted to people who can express their talents and personalities. A highly developed soul will work with us to channel the beautiful aspects of the creative spirit into the world. A less enlightened soul will be drawn to commiserate with us if we are wallowing in self-pity or self-destruction, because misery always loves company. But the last place misery wants to be is in the company of joy, so the best way to keep any negativity far away is to be as balanced and happy as we can.

When we find ourselves in black moods, or amidst the chaos, the cure for our ailing soul is always to embrace love and embrace the divine spirit of joy and goodness. Light dispels the darkness, just as it dispels any negativity we may have inadvertently attracted to us. If we find that we are receiving any impressions from our intuition that have a harmful or negative intent, then we must disregard them and focus on surrounding ourselves with love and balance. It is up to us to choose the company we keep.

For just as we travel with our kindred spirits in this material world, our kindred spirits (literally) travel with us in the immaterial world. This is the Law of Attraction. Like attracts like. We have something in common with everyone we share our lives with, whether it is a common interest, a common personality trait, or job, or goal. This works on both a creative and destructive level. Our acquaintances may join us in fostering our growth, or in contributing to our destructive tendencies. It is up to us to decide with whom we want to spend our time, and whether we want to spend our energy creatively or destructively.

We may choose to heed our guides and make creative choices, or we may choose to exercise our free will and make choices that may not always be in the best interest of our higher selves. Just remember that as we make these choices and live our lives, we will attract nothing to us that is not already inside of us. For us to attract love and goodness, we must cultivate love and goodness within ourselves; if we are attracting fear and negativity, we must find the source of this chaos within ourselves, and release it. Our external world is but a reflection of what lives inside of us.

It is essential for us, as we begin to seek truth, to understand the nature of the metaphysical world as much as possible. The more we understand the energies that exist around us, the more we will be able to work with them confidently. This is especially true for mediumship, when we open ourselves up to communication from immaterial souls. In many ways, spirit communication is a lot like our everyday communication. If we connect with a soul who is full of joy and love, our own spirits are uplifted. On the other hand, if we connect with a soul who is harboring negative emotions, those emotions may bring us down if we do not protect ourselves. Moods rub off—person to person and soul to soul.

As our enlightenment grows, we will find that we live more of our lives in the spirit of love, and less of our lives in fear. Every failure is only a redirection toward a different success; every loss a lesson; every change an opportunity for new life. The longer we live in this spirit, the more naturally centered we become. Inner balance is the by-product of walking in truth.

Our intuition is the beacon that guides us to peace and navigates us through the treacherous karmic waters. No matter how dark it gets, or how rough the ride, or how deep we sink, the light remains constant. We can follow it or we can go our own way. The choice is ours. But it will always be there for us to turn to, even in our darkest hours.

Mystics understand the roots of the Tao, but not its branches;
Scientists understand its branches but not its roots.
Science does not need mysticism and mysticism does not need science.
But man needs both.

—*Fritjof Capra,* The Tao of Physics

CHAPTER 5

MIND EQUALS MATTER: *The Science of Mysticism*

It is not unusual for people to hear terminology like *telepathy, precognition,* or *extrasensory perception (ESP)* and recoil at the thought of such spooky, occult subject matter. Past notions of doomsday prophets spring to mind, along with images of charlatans, "gypsies," and fortunetellers, and the legacies of witch-hunts, cults, and deceivers of the masses. These archaic stereotypes fuel the onslaught of "scientific" researchers on their crusade to debunk these mysterious, unexplainable phenomena. While a true understanding of psychic phenomena has consistently eluded the traditional religious and scientific communities, recent advances in technology and physics are paving the way to a new metaphysical understanding of reality.

The paths of religion and science are converging. The gap between what we feel and what we can measure is narrowing by the decade. True science and true religion are destined only to reinforce each other. After all, truth is truth, whether we can quantify it with technological instruments or simply understand it through the most amazing and mysterious instrument we know of—the human body.

But truth will always have its enemies. People will always have their reasons for not wanting to believe in life after death, or the possibility of interaction between our world and the world beyond. Some people fear the idea. Some people want to forget about it. Some people never want to think about it to begin with; others are more comfortable believing that the end is the end, with no consequences, no more suffering, just a quiet nothingness. Most people who don't believe in an afterlife don't *want* to believe in an afterlife. Many fears and misunderstandings about the nature of the spiritual world prevent people from opening their minds to the reality that death is, in actuality, a joyful homecoming.

Whether we believe in life after death or not, science is already speaking for itself on the matter. We already know that energy cannot be destroyed. It can only be transformed. In the simplest terms, nothing that has been created can ever cease to exist; it can only change. And so we change. We emerge from microscopic interactions of cells and DNA, grow to the physical form we know in this world, and then shed that form, like a butterfly emerges from its chrysalis, to fly home. We were created before this life, and we will exist after this life. We, like all other things in creation, exist eternally, in tandem with the rhythm of the expanding and contracting universe, with the beating heart of our creator.

When we ponder the scientific mysteries of the universe, we must remind ourselves of the humble nature of our understanding. After all, it was only 500 years ago that we thought our solar system revolved around the earth. Imagine the burden of poor, tortured Copernicus, who had to break it to the world, and worse, the church, that humankind was not the center of the universe. And he had to do that despite the fact that the measurable phenomena of the previous ages went against his theory. Every evening, century after century, human beings watched the sun and the planets take their place in the celestial parade across the heavens; the stars rose and set as if the entire production revolved around our little planet.

But as we looked closer, using instruments more advanced than our eyes, and as we began to plot the mathematical charts, we learned that this parade was not all that it would seem. There were anomalies and retrograde motions that simply were not consistent with more than 1,500 years of indoctrinated science. Try telling that to the fourteenth century. It's no surprise that Copernicus was reluctant to go public with his theory. He discreetly circulated his ideas among his peers in 1514, but did not agree to print them publicly until 1540, in the last years of his life.

The scientific community was in shock. This changed everything. This heralded a new world. To the fourteenth century, the idea that the earth wasn't the center of the universe was revolutionary. But today we see that as common knowledge, often sneering at the naiveté of our ancestors. The birth pains of a new idea have long been forgotten. So it has been throughout history. And so it is today, in our process of cultural evolution. Change brings revolution; revolutionary ideas become the norm. Ideas that may seem radical today will one day be a common part of life.

Mysticism is no exception. One day, the reality of life after death may be so commonplace that denying it would be much like someone today denying that the earth is a sphere. But only time will tell. There is a scientific explanation for all mystical experience; we just don't have it yet. Mystical experience abides by the same natural laws of the universe as our physical world. We process psychic information in specific parts of our brain, just as we process other external stimuli. Many psychics have subjected themselves to hours of laborious tests and analyses to help the scientific community better understand how this spiritual process unites with our physiology.

In many cultures, mysticism has evolved hand in hand with science. India, historically, has prided itself both on its spirituality and its scientific prowess. The Buddhist and Hindu religions were founded on mystical elements that have been a part of everyday living for thousands of years. Many of our own culture's greatest scientists, including Johannes Kepler and Albert Einstein, had deep spiritual convictions. Their spirituality and their science reinforced each other; they did not negate each other.

During recent years we have seen a resurgence of this notion in the West, particularly with the advent of Einstein's Theory of Relativity and the development of quantum physics. The profound and unfathomable nature of this new era in science marries well with many aspects of spirituality. The universe is no longer a three-dimensional model of ups and downs, objects and space, somethings and nothings; it is all interconnected, a vast, contradictory web in which everything is relative to perception, and time and space lose meaning as we know them.

Relativity has also made us aware of just how similar matter and energy are—simply two different forms of the same thing. This is most profoundly illustrated in the dynamics between the physical and spiritual worlds. Our bodies are composed of matter; our souls are composed of energy. This was once thought to be a duality; two opposites irreconcilably bound together. But, now, we see that it is otherwise. The matter of our bodies and the energy of our souls are, in fact, just different manifestations of a single underlying whole. Our body is the material extension, or densification, of our spirit. On earth, matter is our reality. We need to touch, see, hear, smell, or taste it in order to accept it. In the spiritual dimensions, energy is the reality. Spirit friends, angels, departed loved ones, the Holy Spirit—all interact in terms of energy.

However, these energies still have different vibrational levels, though none are as dense as that of the physical world. Naturally, the lower vibrating energies will be the ones that most naturally interface with us while we're in our material bodies. Since the material world is a manifestation of a denser expression of energy, purely spiritual beings must lower the frequency of their energy vibration in order to interact with us. Their natural energy frequency is so high that it is imperceptible to our senses. Animals operate at a slightly different vibrational level, often perceiving what we do not. The classic example of the dog whistle illustrates how limited our human faculties are; there is no denying that the sound is there, but we hear nothing.

Naturally, we can conclude that, if we want to enhance our bandwidth of perception, we can do so by expanding our energy vibration to a level closer to the energy that we aim to perceive. This may sound ludicrous at first, but it is truly the most simple and beautiful of concepts. It is generally accepted that the closer an energy is to the divine source, the higher its vibration will be. So, the spiritual hierarchy unfolds, with humanity somewhere in the middle of it all. With the divine source being the highest possible expression and vibration of energy, it only follows that, by embracing the qualities of God, we will become more like God. We all know these qualities: Love. Truth. Faith. Trust. Compassion. Forgiveness. More love. The more we evolve and raise our spirit level with love and wisdom, the easier it is to connect with the spiritual realm.

The spiritual world is all around us. Connecting to it is not a matter of location, or proximity; it does not exist in some distant, faraway place. It is everywhere; it is throughout our world, and it is beyond our world. It is in the space between our houses, our thoughts, our pasts, and our futures. We live in bodies that limit our perception to only those things within the proximity of our five senses; but by tapping into our "sixth sense," we begin to experience the unseen world that exists in the dimensions that overlap our own.

This sixth sense, also called our intuition, is our link to these higher realms of perception. There is a part of our mind that continually interfaces with the higher planes of existence. In this regard, it is our higher self that has access to all of the information that we, in the limited perception of our physical bodies in linear time and space, do not. This is the part of us that just "knows" things, like when the phone will ring, or when someone is hurt, or when to double-check that the coffeepot is turned off. From the simplest everyday matters to the deepest life situations, our intuition guides us in ways that are beyond reason and beyond measure.

Our intuition is our best friend. It is the light in the darkness, the truth behind the lies, our protection in times of danger, our solace in times of sorrow. When we learn to trust our intuition, we gain truth, understanding, and a sense of safety and comfort. When we say that our intuition connects us with the higher spiritual planes, we mean that it also connects us to the love and divinity inherent in those planes. This inner guidance is always there, for everyone. Quietly it nudges us to heed its call, to make the right choices, to better ourselves, and to share the love with others.

It is always shocking to meet life where we thought we were alone . . . "Look out!" we cry, "It's alive!" And therefore this is the very point at which so many draw back . . . An impersonal God—well and good. A subjective God of beauty, truth and goodness, inside our own heads—better still. A formless life force surging through us—best of all. But God, himself, alive, pulling at the other end of the cord, perhaps approaching at infinite speed . . . that is quite another matter.

—*C. S. Lewis,* A Year with C. S. Lewis

CHAPTER 6

OUR INVISIBLE FRIENDS: *Spiritual Beings among Us*

As we begin to get a grasp of the spiritual reality that pervades our life, we quite often struggle with the notion of individual, living beings coexisting with us quite imperceptibly. It is easy for us to imagine angelic beings dwelling in a distant Heaven, somewhere in the faraway ethers, but real beings here—right next to us—with distinct personalities, with talents and interests, who like to laugh and joke like "regular" people . . . that is a different story.

Our spirit friends, many of them, truly are quite "regular." They are, simply, people without bodies. Our departed loved ones retain their unique and distinct personalities, despite their lack of physical form. The primary difference is that they are no longer confined to the limited physical plane of existence, or the boundaries that their personalities imposed upon that existence. They are, in many ways, expanded versions of the people we knew here in this life. They are the people we knew, and so much more. They still live, and love, and experience the created world; they still have companions, and remain our companions. The afterworld is *personal.*

It is this personal, loving world that overlaps with our own, and is home to the beings who are dedicated to the assistance of our earthly missions. Whether we are aware of them or not, we all have a group of spiritual guardians who live and evolve with us throughout our lives. Some people call them guardian angels; others call them spirit guides. Regardless of the name we choose for them, they are with us, guiding us and inspiring us through life's ups and downs. We may think that we have never met these beings, but they are closer to us than our dearest earthly friends. They are our *spiritual* family.

In this life, we might have inherited the physiology that creates a beautiful singing voice. In the same way, our guides share our characteristics and qualities, but on the spiritual level. If we are talented singers, we are likely to have a musically inclined guide who helps us to channel and inspire our own musical talents in the physical world. Much like our earthly parents, our spiritual guardians have our best interests in mind. They are with us to guide us and to help us evolve, but they also learn with us as we shape ourselves through our choices. In this way, our guides are distinctly connected with our higher self. They work with us from a higher perspective to help us make the best decisions with our life. They are secretly our best friends. They grow as we grow. Our triumphs are their triumphs.

Getting to know these beings can be a fascinating process. Though the kinds of spiritual beings that exist in creation are as diverse and unique as the many different forms of life that we know here on earth, our friends and guides on the other side are not very different from our friends here. When we develop our intuition, we can learn to communicate with our spiritual companions, and get to know them just as we would get to know people in our material world. We start a conversation. We listen. We take the time to get to know them, and ourselves in the process.

The generally accepted theory regarding the nature of our spiritual guardians is that they, unlike angels, who are higher entities in the divine hierarchy, are of the relatively same nature as human beings. Most of them have lived human lives, possibly even lives with us. Nonetheless, these are beings who have evolved to a level that enables them to serve as teachers and helpers to the rest of us. They are close enough to us in their spirit level to be able to give to us the guidance and love of the divine way. They may also interact with our loved ones who have passed on. These loved ones often work with our guides to help us and comfort us after their transition, even though we may not be consciously aware of it. In the lives of most people, heavenly assistance goes unnoticed; our guides work selflessly behind the scenes.

Though we usually have a core group of guardians who stay with us throughout our entire lives, many different types of guides and teachers can assist us at different times. Most contemporary spiritual schools categorize different types of guides by the roles they play in our lives. It would seem that our spiritual companions all have their own purpose in our lives. Similarly, we have unique and different relationships with each of our companions, just as we do with our companions in this life.

We do not only interact with our spiritual family *externally*, in space and time, but we also interact with them *internally,* soul to soul. For example, if spiritual beings are in a position to protect us from danger, they can:

1. **Protect us physically:** For example, if we are in a car accident but it is not a time when our souls can afford to be seriously injured, they may protect our bodies during the crash; they may physically move our bodies to the parts of the car where we will receive the least amount of damage.

2. **Protect us via serendipity:** In a similar case, they may help us to avoid the accident altogether by allowing us to forget our wallet, or make a wrong turn, or decide to travel a different route, thus making us late so that we miss the potential situation entirely.
3. **Protect us via inner guidance:** In situations where we must fight our fights ourselves, they infuse us with the courage, the fortitude, or the inner calm we need to overcome our obstacles. Whenever we find ourselves in those moments of unprecedented strength or resolve, we can be sure that our guardians are standing right behind us, and a part of us knows it.

In a very real way, we are influenced by the spiritual company we keep. We absorb the temperaments of our companions in the invisible world just as we do here. Some friends lift our spirits, some friends inspire us, and some friends teach us. Whatever their role, all of our spiritual friends share their gifts with us and seek to elevate us to a level where we will be liberated of our earthly vices.

The following roles of our spiritual companions often referred to as our "guardian angels," demonstrate the many ways these beings help us on a daily basis:

Personal or Joy Guide

As our closest spiritual companion, this being is with us more than most others, knows all of our inner workings, and helps us deal with our everyday matters. Because they are so close to us, they serve as a link to all of the other beings and energies in the spiritual realm. They "keep the gates" between the two worlds by helping us to balance the activities of our higher selves with those of our earthly selves. They also help us keep the "joy" in our lives, to remember to play, to laugh, to keep our inner child alive. We feel the presence of this guide most strongly in the moments when our spirits are unfettered and our souls are alight.

Protectors

We may encounter souls with very interesting earthly histories serving as our protectors. American Indians, Vikings, Roman soldiers, and martial artists are commonly witnessed. Such a concept may seem strange at first, but these are the individuals who have mastered their bravery and their strength while they were on earth, and who, naturally, would be best suited to assist us in the mastery of those same elements during our own trials here. They are like our big brothers, always watching out for us, ready to defend us or rescue us from harm, both physically and spiritually, while also helping us to find the strength to protect ourselves.

Doctors and Teachers

These fascinating beings are our spiritual physicians and teachers. They are often beings of a higher vibration, highly evolved. They work with us to develop our talents and to maintain our emotional, mental, and physical health. They assist us in balancing our hormonal and chemical makeup; they guide us to wisdom, or inspire us to create, or help us make the right choices to heal ourselves. Unlike the protectors and joy guides, whose presence is generally lifelong, doctors and teachers may come and go throughout our lives, depending on the lessons and achievements at hand.

Ascended and Universal Masters

These are individuals who achieved extremely high levels of spiritual evolution on the earthly plane—the saints, the yogis, the holy ones. The ones who have successfully transcended karmic forces and have reached a state of enlightenment. They assist us with self-mastery and help us to evolve through our own karmic destinies and to bring greater good into the world. These beings are at the highest level of human spiritual evolution, and are the purest manifestation of the Holy Spirit that humankind has known. The supreme example of mastery is Christ, whose unwavering manifestation of divine will and love serves as a spiritual beacon for humanity and helps us to transcend the human condition.

It is possible to experience all of these beings in a very personal way. We have heard of people who insist they have seen Jesus in a vision or a dream. Are they mad? Maybe, but maybe not. Christ, in that respect, is like Santa Claus—he can deliver to all of us at the same time. Time is not linear on the other side, so spiritual beings are not racing around trying to get to everyone, one after the other. They have the ability to be anywhere, any time, because they operate outside of time. This is how each of us is able to have the most personal experience with God, with the Eternal One who cares about each one of us and has an infinite amount of time and attention for us all.

Our spiritual family is but a thought away. Think of them, and they are there. Travel is, on the spiritual plane, a matter of thought, not of distance or time. Our thoughts are our connection. We send out our thoughts to the heavens, and our intuition brings the heavenly direction back to us. Whether or not we consciously embrace our spiritual family, they will work with us all the same. It is not necessary for us to know them in order to use our intuition, or to develop our intuitive ability. However, understanding our intuition is the best way to help them help us.

Religion is for those who don't want to go to Hell.
Spirituality is for those who have already been through it.

—*Anonymous*

CHAPTER 7

SIGNS: *How the Spiritual World Gets Our Attention*

We don't have to live in Hollywood to experience the drama of the supernatural world. The mystery of the unexplained has touched all of our lives, whether we acknowledge it or not—strange creaks in the walls, quirky electronic devices, unexplained coincidences, and so on. Most inexplicable happenings are simply natural by-products of living in a spiritual world. When we acknowledge that the world of our existence is both physical and spiritual, we can rationally, calmly accept the external spiritual phenomena that occur in our lives.

This is the beauty about souls in the spiritual dimension: They can communicate with us *internally,* through our intuition, guiding us, nudging our consciences or inspiring us to action; or, because they are distinct living beings in their own right, they can communicate with us *externally,* with physical manifestations of their presence. Examples of this kind of manifestation are endless.

Our friends in the spirit world have limitless means to get our attention, or to give us messages and affirmations. They know that, occasionally, we all need external guidance, a sign that we are on the right track, or making the right decision, or that things will get better for us. Many people will begin to tune into these kinds of events after a loved one has passed on. Loved ones, just like our guides, often go to great lengths to give us reassurance of their well-being after death, or to comfort us as we grieve our loss of them.

Because the spiritual body is essentially one of *energy,* spiritual beings can easily manipulate electronic devices. One of the most common means of communication is through instruments such as radios, telephones, lights, or anything else controlled by electricity. A sign can be as simple as a flickering light or as meaningful as turning our radios on to a song with a specific message for us. Streetlights may happen to turn off, or on, just as we drive by. The phone may ring with no one on the other end of the line. We may find special objects moved about, or in our path, to get our attention. Gifts may be left for us, with no apparent sender. Our attention may be drawn to significant words on license plates, or buses, or road signs—words that may have meaning or direction for us. We may even see lights or apparitions, or feel a touch on our skin. We may have vivid dreams that offer us guidance or comfort. Everything in our life provides a way for Heaven to communicate with us. Even the movies we watch, the books we read, and the conversations we have with people can give us answers to our questions if we are observant enough to notice.

When our guides or loved ones reach out to us, their intention is not to scare us—though this often ends up being the case. Our fears often get in the way of the guidance or consolation we are being offered. When we are fortunate enough to have direct experience with the unseen forces, we should not be afraid. Instead, we should try to understand the purpose of the experience. Did the light flicker at an important point during a conversation? Did the song that I happened to hear on the radio five different times today carry any special message or meaning for me? If we take the time to try to put the puzzle pieces together, we can begin, at last, to see the big picture.

So, the next time you hear a bump in the night, you don't need to pull the covers up over your head; maybe you only need to say "hello." Most of the time, this is just someone's way of saying hello to us, in the only way they know how. Souls who have made their transition to the spirit world often still long to communicate with us. They want us to know they are all right and are still among us. Our inability to perceive them can be frustrating for them, and so they may go to great lengths to make contact with us. We must never think that we are alone, or have been forgotten by our loved ones who have passed on. Chances are they are right next to us, calling out to our deaf ears. Maybe it is time for us to do the "other" world a favor, and start listening.

As we do so, we will slowly begin to realize how connected we are with the greater spiritual whole, and we will learn that we have an infrastructure of spiritual support with us always. Never are we alone in our lives. Aloneness is only an illusion of the material world, a world of separation of things by other things. In the spiritual realm, there is no physical separation, for there is no space between us, and there is no time to keep us apart.

PART TWO

DISCOVERING INNER GUIDANCE:
Developmental Workshops

Love takes up where knowledge leaves off.

—*Saint Thomas Aquinas*

Intuition is the soul's power of knowing God.

—Paramahansa Yogananda

CHAPTER 8

DIVINE INTUITION: *How Psychic Awareness Functions in Our Lives*

Once we understand that it is possible for the spiritual and material worlds to interact, we can begin to use this understanding consciously in our lives. We have established that we understand information from the spirit world via our intuition, or our sixth sense. The next step is to learn to recognize the intuitive information that we receive on a daily basis. When we do this:

1. We begin to have experiences that validate our belief in the continuity of life after death.
2. We begin to make better life choices as our intuition grows stronger, which gives us a new sense of inner peace and comfort.

When we live in tune with our higher self we are less harried by indecision and less likely to make poor choices, to overlook things, or to be insensitive. This is because we are developing our perceptiveness. *Extra*-sensory perception develops from a general lifestyle of perceptiveness. We become more aware of what is actually going on around us, both overtly and behind the scenes. We may not have all of the facts, but our "gut" feeling serves us well.

When we begin to cultivate our intuition, many areas of our life become enriched, and many processes come to us with a newfound ease.

Intuition Is Your Silent Helper

Forget about the pros and the cons. When we turn to our intuition, we may simply "know" or "feel" the best course for ourselves. Which house to buy? What subject to study? Who to give our hearts to? No amount of rational decision-making can counteract the certainty of a strong intuition. To become more aware of this kind of inner guidance, we should listen to our instincts, and take the small chances that may sometimes be contrary to our normal reasoning. For example, if we feel inclined to take an alternative route to work one day, we have little to lose by trying it. Who knows what traffic congestion or accidents we may be avoiding along the way? With time, these little steps of trust will be validated, and we can learn to have faith in the reason behind our intuition.

Planning

When should we take a vacation? Or schedule a lunch date with a friend? Our higher self assists us well as we make our plans because it is aware of everything that is going on, everywhere. Our higher self has access to all of the unseen factors and situations that contribute to the outcomes we desire. If we rely on our intuition when we look forward to future events, we can spare ourselves a good amount of aggravation and disappointment. Our intuitive feelings can give us clues as to whether we should count on something or begin preparing Plan B.

Creativity

Inspiration. Music. Art. Literature. Design. Choreography. The desire to express ourselves creatively, in any form, is a fundamental element of human nature. When we are inspired, when we feel creative, we are allowing ourselves to take part in one of the most divine processes: We create, just as we were created. Our intuition taps into this wonderful source of endless inspirational power; the more we open to our intuition, the more our creativity will flow.

Health

Our body speaks to us in many ways. When not speaking to us through its most obvious language—pain—it speaks to us through our energy levels, our wellness, even our cravings. We crave what our body needs. We may find ourselves craving orange juice or spicy food when our body is fighting off a cold, or we may want red meat if we are anemic. A craving is one means for our higher self to help maintain physiological balance. We may also have intuitions about our health. For instance, you may suddenly feel motivated to go to the dentist, and then find out that you have a cavity.

We may feel blockages or sensations in problem areas—symptoms that, at one time, might have escaped our awareness. There are many ways that our intuition will assist us in maintaining our health. It is important to be aware of our intuition's messages, and to seek medical attention when necessary.

Relationships

The most interesting experiences (and challenges) in our lives come in the form of our personal relationships. It is through other people that we confront ourselves. Some relationships may be a source of suffering, and some may be a source of boundless joy. Some relationships assist us in our self-evolution. Others may assist us better if we abandon them. Our intuition is the gauge that allows us to understand the depths and meaning of our friendships, our loves, and even our colleagues. Our intuition will key us in to those who have our best interests in mind, as well as those who do not. Intuition is above dishonesty, for it senses the truth behind any deception. It doesn't always tell us what we want to hear, so heeding it may not always be as easy as we think.

Finances

When we buy something, we almost always know right off the bat if our newest acquisition is going to prove to be a smart one. When we were making that decision—*is this for me?*—we were receiving tiny nudges to clue us in to the answer. Sometimes we will be sure to talk ourselves into something: *This would be so good for me.* Meanwhile, we keep overruling the nagging sensation that this might not be such a good idea. If we pay attention to our intuition, and don't make the purchase, we usually feel relieved and are sure of our choice to pass on the object in question. On the other hand, if we override our intuition, we will certainly find that hindsight is 20/20: The car turned out to be a lemon. The boots were too small. The part doesn't fit. Our intuition can save us a good deal of frustration, and money, if we use it wisely.

While many of these areas may seem to be mundane uses for our intuition, more extraordinary manifestations will occur with time and experience.

Telepathy and Precognition

Two very common types of intuitive phenomena are telepathy and precognition. We just *know* something, even with no rational justification. How often do we think of someone who, moments later, calls on the phone? How often do we find ourselves knowing what people are going to say before they speak? This "telepathic" or "mind-to-mind" communication occurs when the higher selves of two individuals connect before direct, conscious interaction takes place. Our intuition opens the pathway between our higher selves and our conscious selves, therefore allowing us to experience the thought energy of others before it is translated into words or actions.

Similarly, the act of precognition occurs when our intuition provides us with information regarding events and life circumstances that have not yet manifested or come into our personal circle of awareness. Maybe we just *know* that Kelly is going to find a treasure at the flea market on Tuesday. Or we just have this sneaking suspicion that Scott is finally going to buy that house he's been talking about. This kind of intuition may simply come to us as a subtle sense of "knowing," or in more dramatic ways that include actual physical sensations or vivid dreams. Either way, our intuition is alerting us to situations that may require our attention or understanding. From the simplest matters of life to the most complex matters of the soul, our intuition is our unwavering source of certainty.

> *Trust your instinct to the end, though you can render no reason.*
>
> *—Ralph Waldo Emerson*

Chapter 9

First Impressions Never Lie: *The Three-Step Process of Intuitive Awareness*

The first impression is the purest impression. It is our instantaneous reaction to a person or situation—a reaction that is usually unfettered by our expectations, fears, or responsibilities. We are provided with a stimulus, and we have an immediate response or feeling; this is our intuition at work. The next response is to integrate that impression into our understanding; this is our rational mind at work. In this way, our intuitive mind (right brain) works together with our rational mind (left brain) to form a synthesis of understanding.

Our higher self endows us with the flash of insight we commonly call a first impression. Though we may know very little about a person or situation, we may get a very distinct "vibe" about the nature of things. For example, we may get a bad feeling about a certain venture, for no apparent reason. Or we may meet someone for the first time, and feel that we have known them before. At that point, we attempt to understand the meaning of our impression, to determine if that "vibe" fits our reality. So begins the reign of the rational mind. If we trust our first impressions, we try to understand how they fit into the scheme of things. If we doubt those impressions, we often find out later that we chose to deceive ourselves.

When it comes to our intuition, we must trust our higher selves as much as possible. When we become aware of intuitive information, we immediately find ourselves asking, *Is this real? Does this make sense? Is this just my imagination?* To understand the answer to these questions, we should understand what an intuitive impression feels like, and what it is like to receive information from the spirit world.

Intuitive impressions feel like thoughts that just come to mind. We all have them, every day of our lives. They occur as passing ideas or images, often as reminders or suggestions about situations in our lives. To better recognize them, we should pay attention to any ideas that spring to mind, often out of the blue. We may suddenly think about someone, only to have that person walk through our door just moments later; we may have the impulse to stop for groceries, only to have an unexpected dinner guest show up that night. These are examples of how our intuition works with us naturally in our daily activities. Once we are tuned in to them on this level, we can take our awareness to the higher levels. We may begin to sense when a person has done something wrong, before anything is said. We may find ourselves serendipitously being in the right places at the right times. We may foresee trends in our life, or the lives of others, before they manifest. We may instinctively know what is good for us and what is detrimental for us, without justifiable reason.

Our intuition omnipotently links us with the objective state of the world, allowing us to transcend our own subjective reality.

It provides us with higher awareness, if we choose to acknowledge it. It is the line of communication to our higher selves and to other souls who are living, but not in physical form. We can communicate with them mind to mind, thought to thought.

It is not surprising, then, that intuitive impressions may often feel like our own thoughts, because they *are* thoughts, just like our own. The primary difference is that intuitive thoughts originate externally, from the higher sources, instead of being born within our own conscious minds. We actively create our own conscious thoughts; we passively receive intuitive thoughts.

 Intuition Workshop

Becoming Aware of Intuition

When we understand how the intuitive process works, we may begin to solicit inner guidance at will. By allowing our intuition a voice in our decision-making and reactions to everyday situations, we can create a more balanced perspective on life.

Tips for Recognizing Intuition

When you begin working with your intuition, keep some of the following ideas in mind:

- Be as objective as possible. If you are attached to a specific outcome, or if you have your own hopes or fears regarding the information you receive, your own mind will get in the way of any objective guidance.
- Don't force it. If you listen too hard or focus on your expectations, you will generate a mental static that prevents you from recognizing anything at all.

- Pay attention. Responses from Heaven often come instantaneously. Sometimes they come so quickly that you may miss them altogether. If you do miss a response, you should relax and try to let it come to you again.

The Three-Step Process of Intuition

The process of intuitive understanding is essentially a process of *communication.* Heaven responds to us, and we respond to Heaven, though not necessarily in that order.

1. **Stimulus:** An intuitive stimulus is anything, any thought, action, event, or person, that causes a psychic impression. We can initiate this process consciously, by asking for guidance or for spiritual information, or we can take part in it passively, in those cases when Heaven gives us impressions spontaneously.

2. **Response:** This is Heaven's response to the earthly thought, event, or query that prompts our intuition. This is the process by which we receive inner guidance or psychic information. The response generally will come as our first impression after the stimulus.

3. **Synthesis:** These are many thoughts that follow our first impression. These are generally products of our rational mind integrating the response with our reality. These thoughts can also be intuitively guided, and may assist us with understanding the higher meaning of the impression. The synthesis is a process of balancing and integrating our rational and intuitive understanding of the information we received.

CASE STUDY #1: Women's Intuition

1. **Stimulus:** A young woman sees her boyfriend talking with another woman.

2. **Response:** The woman gets a distinct feeling of distrust toward the other woman.
3. **Synthesis:** Despite denial on both the man's and the other woman's part, the young woman determines that they are not being forthright about the true nature of their situation.

Note: At this point the woman's free will comes into play, because she has the choice to heed this impression or deny it, and make her decisions accordingly.

CASE STUDY #2: Heavenly Reminders

1. **Stimulus:** A man who is recovering from the flu lights up a cigarette.
2. **Response:** The thought of a stop sign pops into his mind.
3. **Synthesis:** He determines that his sickness will probably be prolonged by his continued smoking.

Note: At this point the man's free will comes into play, because he has the choice to put out the cigarette or to continue and take the risk of damaging his health.

CASE STUDY #3: Psychic Tip-offs

1. **Stimulus:** The phone rings at a woman's house.
2. **Response:** Her sister's name pops into her mind.
3. **Synthesis:** She wonders if her sister could be calling on the phone.

Note: Impressions like this are extremely helpful, because they are immediately verifiable, unlike the previous two cases, which may take weeks or months to validate.

To successfully integrate higher awareness into our lives, we should strive to react to our impressions in as balanced a way as possible. We must differentiate between true inner guidance and false hopes and fears. For example, the woman in Case Study #1 must be able to differentiate a genuine impression about her boyfriend's infidelity from any paranoid fears she might be open to entertaining. It is important to remember that *pure intuition is given in a spirit of quiet knowing and acceptance*. When we understand a situation with our higher selves, we are more inclined to allow ourselves to accept the divine order, even if the subject matter is distressing or goes against our personal objectives.

Frequently Asked Questions

Question: "I sometimes get impressions in the form of a statement or command that refers to me personally. For example, if I react poorly to a situation, thoughts like 'You should know better, my friend' often spring to mind. What does that mean?"

Explanation: When we begin to register these kinds of impressions, we have most likely initiated a dialogue with one of the souls who guide us.

Suggestion: Try talking back!

Question: "Sometimes I get silly or strange impressions. Is that normal?"

Explanation: We should not be surprised if we occasionally receive colorful or humorous impressions. Heaven *does* have a sense of humor. Our guardians and friends on the other side all have their unique personalities and may enjoy expressing themselves with jokes, irony, sarcasm, or even a general sense of playfulness. Regardless of the tone of their individual personalities, our guides will only assist us on our path in a nurturing, life-affirming spirit.

Suggestion: Lighten up and enjoy the humor.

Question: "I received an impression that really upset me. What should I do?"

Explanation: Chances are that if you received an impression that caused you significant emotional distress, you did not receive a genuine impression at all. Emotionally charged impressions are generally manifestations of your own thought processes based on your fears. You may be too close to the situation to be able to approach it objectively. Emotional attachment is like intuitive kryptonite. Our unbalanced emotions create a static energy around us that interferes with the intuitive process.

Suggestion: Reapproach the situation selflessly, with a clear mind. Release any personal attachment to the outcome of the situation. If this is not possible, do not attempt further intuitive work at this time.

Summary

After reading and understanding this three-step process, learn to recognize it in your own life. Ask specific questions of yourself and notice Heaven's response. Become more aware of the impressions you get from day-to-day situations.

Our intuition serves us like a weather vane, pointing us in the right direction. It does not make our decisions for us. A policy of noninterference, a kind of spiritual prime directive, is at work in the ethers: We are to live our lives for ourselves. Our choices are ours to make. Our connections in the metaphysical world may only assist us in this process, much as a friend in this world would. They can affirm our thoughts on certain matters, reinforce our aspirations, provide encouragement, offer understanding or hope, and, of course, help us to enjoy our lives.

Experience is never limited, and it is never complete; it is an immense sensibility, a kind of huge spider-web of the finest silken threads suspended in the chamber of consciousness, and catching every air-borne particle in its tissue.

—*Henry James*

CHAPTER 10

SENSE AND META-SENSIBILITY: *Intuition and the Psychic Senses*

The universe is filled with an incomprehensible amount of energy and substance, most of which is imperceptible to our physical senses. Radio waves, microwaves, infrared light, and microscopic particles are just a few examples of the infinite aspects of reality that elude the perception of the five senses. In essence, our senses serve as a filter, allowing us to experience what is most necessary for our physical existence. The five senses create the set for the stage we call our lives.

The range of perception created by the senses can be expanded by fine-tuning our physical and spiritual awareness. Hence the term *extrasensory perception*; we learn to perceive beyond the normal ranges of the five senses. And how can we do this? By utilizing our five *meta-senses,* collectively referred to as the sixth sense:

1. clairvoyance (sight)
2. clairaudience (sound)

3. clairsentience (feeling)
4. clairambience (smell)
5. clairalience (taste)

Each meta-sense (meaning "beyond" sense) corresponds to one of the five senses, and functions with the same essential nature. The difference is that the meta-senses are experienced in our spiritual body, as opposed to our physical body.

Our intuition works in conjunction with these five meta-senses to enable heavenly communication. The information that is input through our psychic senses is processed through our intuitive understanding. Just as our rational mind recognizes the meaning of the things we see, hear, or feel through the physical senses, our intuitive mind recognizes the meaning of impressions received through the psychic senses. Our intuition also may provide us with information without any input from the meta-senses. We may just simply "know" things, for no reason at all.

Though there are times when the spiritual realm will manifest directly to our five physical senses, most often we work with the unseen forces by using the five extrasensory channels. We utilize these meta-senses every night when we dream. As many of us know, the intensity and sensations of dreams often are indistinguishable from those of reality.

It should come as no surprise, then, to learn that we can use our psychic senses consciously in a kind of controlled "daydream" state. When psychics "see" things that no one else can, they are generally seeing through their mind's eye, abstractly. This is generally metaphysical sight, not the work of our eyeballs. This is clairvoyance. The same is true when we perceive metaphysical sounds. Though voices can be loud and clear in our mind, with distinct accents, tones, and gender, they are not (they can be *actually* heard with the ears occasionally) heard with our ears. The stimulus that we receive does not originate in the material world. Intuitive impressions, like thoughts, originate from the inside, from the metaphysical dimension. It is also not unusual to perceive smells or tastes or distinct physical or emotional feelings when we are working with the higher forces. The spirit world only expects to communicate with us by presenting us with what we know from our normal, sensory experience.

As we begin to work with our psychic senses, each of us will most likely have a meta-sense, or extrasensory channel, that tunes in more clearly in the beginning. We all have natural receptivity in different areas. When we understand how we receive information, we can begin to work with the energy more effectively. Our physical body is like an antenna that channels, then amplifies that energy. Our task is to figure out what energy we want to bring into this world, then find the right channel to tune in to. We have psychic channels just like we have creative channels, inspirational channels, motivational channels, emotional channels, and so forth. We can turn them on, or we can turn them off. When we turn them on, we can turn the volume up, or leave it at a whisper.

The Five Psychic Senses

Our psychic channels, or meta-senses, work in conjunction with our intuition to provide us with the highest levels of inner guidance. The more we get in touch with our higher selves, the clearer each channel will become. Developing these senses takes time and patience.

Clairvoyance: "Clear Seeing"

- Physical Area of Receptivity: "Third eye," frontal cortex
- Manifestation: Visual symbols and images

Clairvoyant Personality Type

People with a strong clairvoyant channel are often artistic or literary by nature. They tend to process things visually, and have a propensity for metaphor. Writers, artists, designers, and the like spend a good deal of time flexing their visual muscles or communicating through metaphors.

Though there are some people who can actually "see dead people," most of us will experience clairvoyant impressions in the same way that we experience imagination or memory. We can imagine or remember the details of, for example, our car; we can picture that it is a silver Subaru wagon with a hatchback and tinted windows. We are not actually looking at the car, but we are seeing it in our minds. This is the same way we would see a clairvoyant impression; only we would not have *generated* the image ourselves, we would have *received* it. If we receive a clairvoyant impression of a car, the idea of this car just comes to mind. We can see it in our mind's eye—the color, model, condition, and any other pertinent details.

Visual impressions can be symbolic or literal. We may experience "visions" of different scenes or events in the past, present, or future, or we may be given symbols to clue us in to what is happening, or what is to come. For example, if a wedding is in the future, we could be given the information via "remote viewing," which would show us an actual wedding scene in our minds or even reference a wedding that took place in our own lives. We also might be given a symbol to represent a wedding, such as a pair of interlocking gold bands. How we receive the information is not as important as understanding the information. The idea is for the information to come to us in whatever way will make sense to us. This is why we all usually develop our own unique variations of higher communication.

Clairaudience: "Clear Hearing"

- Physical Area of Receptivity: Temporal lobe, the brain's auditory center
- Manifestation: Auditory sound and language

Clairaudient Personality Type

A strongly clairaudient individual will often have a natural affinity toward musical ability, or even mathematics or technology. Information is generally processed linearly, as opposed to spatially. These individuals may also be "good listeners."

The very common example of clairaudience is the song that we have had going through our minds for hours or days. We don't actually *hear* the song, but it keeps running through our minds. It's the *thought* of the song that captures our attention.

Auditory impressions also can be realistic. We may hear actual voices in our heads, often with a specific gender and accent. These are usually the voices of our spirit guides, or of souls in the spiritual realm who intend to deliver a message or guidance. We can hear distinct sounds, music, voices, commands, questions, or instructions, depending on our situation and sensibilities.

Clairsentience: "Clear Sensing"

- Physical Areas of Receptivity: The physical body (physical sensations), the solar plexus (emotions), the corpus collosum (psychic knowing)
- Manifestation: Bodily sensations, emotional states, feelings of "knowing" or "understanding"

Clairsentient Personality Type

The more "sensitive" we are, the more likely we are to use our clairsentience. Those of us who are in touch with our feelings and our emotions will have an easier time accessing these channels than those of us who do not embrace our "feeling" nature.

This psychic sense can manifest through actual physical sensations on or within our bodies, through distinct emotions, or through distinct understandings of situations or events which are typically beyond the parameters of our immediate experience. We may experience actual physical sensations as we work with the spirit realm. We may feel souls "touch" us with their energy; this often feels like slight touches or tingling on our skin. We may also feel subtle pains or sensations anywhere on our bodies. For instance, if a soul is trying to communicate that the body's cause of death was colon cancer, we may feel a slight ache or burning in our abdominal area.

We also may experience clairsentience through our emotions. If a soul is communicating with us, we may temporarily feel their joy, or their sadness, or their general energy level. We would feel this just as we feel our own emotions. Or, sometimes, we may just "know" that something significant is happening to a loved one, even though we may be miles away. We often find ourselves with an inner certainty or understanding that we cannot explain. Our kindred spirits on earth, just like those in spirit, are constantly communicating with us on a higher level, and very often through clairsentience.

Clairambience: "Clear Smelling"

- Physical Area of Receptivity: Olfactory receptors
- Manifestation: A distinct scent or smell, either through memory or actual scent

CLAIRAMBIENT PERSONALITY TYPE

We may experience clairambience as a kind of "ghost" scent. We may smell something when nobody else does. We may smell things like flowers or a perfume when we are in a place where there could be no source for such things. Clairambience can be especially obvious when we are driving in a car, because the contained air space will make unusual scents clear and indisputable. These scents can be so strong that they overwhelm our sense of smell, or they can be so subtle that we just think of the smell. Specific smells are very often associated with the presence of a specific soul. For example, if we always associated our grandmother with her perfume, she might choose to give us, from the spiritual world, the clairambient impression of that scent so that we can identify her presence.

Clairalience: "Clear Tasting"

- Physical Area of Receptivity: Gustatory receptors
- Manifestation: A distinct taste, either through memory or actual taste

Clairalient Personality Type

We experience clairalience very much in the way we experience clairambience, although clairalience is probably the least common of all five meta-senses. Spirits may give us impressions through taste to associate themselves with a special food they were known for, or for any other significant reason. Again, we may experience an actual taste in our mouth, or we may simply be "reminded" of a taste.

One Impression, Five Senses

The following example illustrates how a single impression may be channeled differently through each one of the five meta-senses. Let's say that a soul is trying to identify itself to us. During this process, souls will usually search out traits from their lives that would have specific, unique meaning to us. For instance, let's say that this soul, as a young man, loved to eat lollipops—always had a lollipop with him. We may have joked with him about this on many occasions or bought lollipops for him at one time or another. In such a case, the simplest impression of a lollipop could hold a world of meaning to us. An impression of a lollipop can come through our higher senses in many different ways.

Via Clairvoyance

If we are dominantly clairvoyant we may get a fleeting visual image of a lollipop. If we make the association between our friend and the lollipop, then the mission is accomplished. If we do not make the association, or miss the first impression of the lollipop, our friends on the other side may repeat it for us to drive the point home. We may keep "seeing" this lollipop over and over. If we still do not get it, Heaven may even go so far as to start giving us references to other things that might make us get "lollipop"—for example, they might show us an image of Kojak (with a little giggle, perhaps).

Via Clairaudience

In this case, we could simply hear the word "lollipop," or the word could just pop into our heads. Again, if we miss it, we may get follow-up by hearing references to Kojak, or even "Dum-Dum" or "Tootsie Pops" or whatever.

Via Clairsentience

In this case, we could find ourselves with a strange craving for lollipops. We might get the feeling that it would be great to have a lollipop now, or even find ourselves instinctively picking up a lollipop or two next time we are at the store.

Via Clairambiance

Since we don't usually *smell* lollipops, Heaven may be least likely to use this sense; nonetheless, it wouldn't be unheard of to notice the sweet scent of candy around us in an instance like this.

Via Clairalience

Obviously, in this case, we could get the taste of lollipops or candy in our mouth, or even the thought of how lollipops taste.

The bottom line is that Heaven will use whatever means necessary to get the message across. We could find ourselves using any or all of these senses. As we begin to keep track of the kinds of impressions we receive during our spiritual work, we will be able to determine which senses, or channels, we tune in to better than others. The more we develop our higher senses, the more consistent and clear the information from the spirit world will become. In the beginning, our impressions may be fuzzy. We may only get fragments, much in the way we only hear disjointed bits of information when a radio station isn't tuned in properly. We may only hear random words or bits of information at first, but in time, as the channels become finely tuned, the words become full sentences, full dialogue, and the fragments will attach themselves to meaning.

With time, we will develop the ability to discriminate between the thoughts that are our own and the thoughts that come to us from higher sources. We can become confused when we are first learning to interpret information from the spirit world because impressions may be so familiar to us that they are misinterpreted as memories. For example, if a soul wants to reference a necklace they gave us, we may receive an impression of that necklace, but think we are only remembering it. We may envision all of its details, but we are unable to tell whether we are receiving those details or remembering them. On the other hand, if a reference to that same necklace comes to us from a psychic who knows nothing about us, it becomes a very important validation for a certain soul's continued presence in our life.

If we want to be more aware of the loved ones who are present in our daily lives, we should pay close attention to the direction of our thoughts. Our own thoughts are often a reaction to a soul's presence with us. Sometimes, when we think we have just thought of them, they were really there with us, thinking of us all the while.

Psychic Senses Workshop

Be brave enough to live creatively. The creative is the place where no one else has ever been. You have to leave the city of your comfort and go into the wilderness of your intuition. You cannot get there by bus, only by hard work, risking and by not quite knowing what you are doing. What you will discover will be wonderful: yourself.

—Alan Alda

Understanding the Meta-senses

When we take spiritual wisdom and apply it to a practical application of the intuitive arts, we have much to offer ourselves and others. By actively participating in the metaphysical process, we can be the vessel of objective truths that escape our subjective, conscious minds. We can offer evidence and hope in regard to the continuous structure of life, one that transcends what we call death. We can learn how to live our lives with a calm acceptance of divine will, and help others to do the same.

The following workshop was created to assist in the unfolding of both the beginner and advanced intuitive ability.

These three workshop sessions are formulated to assist us in strengthening our means of meta-sensory communication. The first deals with clairvoyance, the second with clairaudience, and the third with clairsentience (which also includes clairambience and clairalience). Our intuition will guide us to understand the information that we receive from our higher selves and spiritual guardians through our meta-senses.

Tips for Working with the Psychic Senses

Understanding the following ideas will help us as we begin to work with our "psychic senses."

- Remember that the way in which we receive intuitive information is largely out of our control, and depends upon our internal "wiring" or biochemistry. We cannot force visual impressions if we are more inclined to receive auditory impressions, or vice versa.
- Be open to developing any kind of intuitive ability you are given. Work with the sessions that follow in this workshop to determine which types of communications function best for you.
- If you have little luck with one process, move on to another. Not everyone will have success in every area. When we find our area of strength, we can focus on developing it first, then fine-tune our other senses in time.
- Always be aware of spiritual ethics. Always seek information for the purpose of the higher good—for ourselves, as well as others. We should resist any temptation toward "psychic snooping" or using our intuition to attempt to gain personal information about a person, without their consent. Be mindful of spiritual privacy.

- Resist any temptation to show off, or to gratify our egos, once we attain a degree of success in our work. The purpose of our dedication to the intuitive process should always be founded in the search for truth and wisdom, not in our own personal gain.

When we are working successfully with our intuition, we will often feel as if we are "in our zone." Just as with any other creative or physical activity, we may need some time to warm up before we get into the flow of things. Don't be surprised if, during the first few minutes of intuitive work, we feel clumsy or out of sorts; the longer we stay at it, the more open we become, and the better we function. Just as in physical exercise, we need to "warm up" in our spiritual exercise. It usually doesn't take very long for us to get so far into the process that we lose ourselves. This is the ideal. The less of ourselves we have in our psychic process, the better.

Clairvoyance and the Visual Language

Heaven often communicates with us by providing brief flashes of symbolic or familiar images. The meaning of this imagery can very often be quite elusive until we learn to understand the sort of visual language that Heaven uses to interact with us. Many people ask why souls communicate with symbols if they could use words, which clearly function as a more direct means of communication. The answer is as simple as the age-old saying: A picture is worth a thousand words. A clairvoyant picture is often like a painting—a single image full of subtle intricacies of metaphor and symbolism. What would take a considerable amount of time and energy to put into words comes quite simply in the form of a picture.

Session #1: Introduction to Receiving Clairvoyant Impressions

In this session, we will focus on receiving impressions in our mind's eye, via mental pictures or symbols. These impressions will be focused on our lives and any guidance or validations that Heaven chooses to give us in that regard. Validation of information that we had no earthly means of acquiring is the only way to build our confidence and faith in the genuine nature of the intuitive process.

To begin the following session, take a few moments to prepare yourself and balance your thoughts.

Suggestion: Meditate on the development of your mind's eye, and practice envisioning symbols and imagery in your mind. Allow any imagery to flow with your stream of consciousness. This creates fertile mental territory for visual impressions.

1. **Stimulus:** Ask for visual intuitive impressions that you can confirm in your own life. Quietly center yourself and ask Heaven for general guidance or information surrounding your life at the moment, keeping in mind the three-step intuitive process. Do not focus on a particular question, or specifics, but instead on receiving any information that may help you to understand your ability to communicate through clairvoyance. Ask that you will be able to validate any information given to you in the near future, possibly even the same day, or within a week at the most. Ask that Heaven only use your visual language at this time. Leave the subject matter up to Heaven. Open your mind. Have no expectations.

Affirmation: "I am an instrument of Heaven's highest wisdom. Allow me to strengthen my inner vision. Open my eyes to all that God puts before me."

2. **Response:** After affirming your intention to work with your visual language, quiet your mind, and then allow any impressions to flow in. Open yourself to any random images, symbols, colors, or pictures that pop into your mind, however subtle or fleeting. At first, the flow of impressions may be only a trickle, but the more you relax and let go of your self-judgment, the faster it will come. Pay attention to the first impressions that appear in your mind's eye. Most often we will receive them as subtle, fleeting flashes. They may be so fast and intangible that we may wonder if it was a genuine intuitive impression at all. But the fact is that, if you thought of it, it was real. Do not doubt what you receive, no matter how elusive or meaningless the information may initially seem.

Remember: Intuitive impressions feel very similar to memories. Anything you can remember by picturing it in your mind's eye is a potential impression. Simple impressions like stop signs, food items, or objects are typical kinds of impressions that we easily recognize in the beginning of our development. As we progress, we may notice our visual impressions becoming more complex, including places, people, motion, or events. The key is to accept whatever comes to mind, however grand or however seemingly insignificant, without prejudice.

3. **Synthesis:** Once you have become aware of the impression, try to focus on it. A genuine impression will settle in, sometimes repeating itself, or sometimes just remaining constant. The longer you ponder it, the more substantial it should feel. You may also begin to sense other information that will help you get a better sense of what the impression means.

CASE STUDY #1: Information Through Clairvoyance

A woman is on her way to meet a friend for lunch. As she is driving in her car, she asks Heaven for any impressions about the course of her upcoming visit with her friend. One of the first thoughts that pops into her mind is the image of a boy with a ca on his arm. She makes a mental note of the impression, then continues on to lunch, wondering if the impression could mean that one of her friend's sons had broken his arm. After arriving at lunch, she asks how the sons are doing. She is not at all surprised to find out that the older boy had recently broken his wrist in a snowboarding accident.

CASE STUDY #2: Clairvoyant Guidance

A man is traveling to a music store in a mall that he has never visited before. The mall is very large and he does not know where to park in order to be near the particular music store. He decides to ask for guidance as to the best route to enter the mall. The first thought that comes to his mind is an image of the JCPenney logo. He is, at first, a little confused, because he was not looking for JCPenney. As he approaches the mall, he notices that there is, in fact, a JCPenney store in the mall, so he decides to enter there. As he passes through the store, toward its entry to the mall, he notices the sign for the music store directly in front of him. He is delighted as he realizes that he had actually entered the mall at the closest possible entrance to the store.

CASE STUDY #3: Clairvoyant Warnings

As a girl is waking up in the morning, she spontaneously gets an impression of flashing sirens and lights, similar to those on a police car. At first she wonders if it is just her imagination, but then she thinks to herself that perhaps she had better watch her driving that day, just in case. She resolves to drive cautiously and obey the speed limit to avoid any potential traffic tickets. As she rounds a corner where she often finds herself speeding, she abruptly comes upon stopped traffic at the scene of a large accident. If she had been driving recklessly, she may easily have caused another accident.

mpressions can come to us as warnings, as guid- formation, or even simply as validations of the Simple validations like this can help us to build in the genuine truth of the intuitive process. Though there may be times when validations for certain impressions fail to materialize, we should not let this deter our progress. There are many reasons verification eludes us, the most common being that we fail to notice it, or to make the right connection in our mind. By seeking personal validations on a regular basis, we can build our intuitive language and strengthen our perceptive abilities.

Session #2: Receiving Clairvoyant Impressions for Spiritual Guidance

In this session, we will still focus on receiving visual impressions as a source of meaningful guidance for our own lives, and for the lives of others. Visual impressions can help us to understand the nature of our life's circumstances, and provide us with clues about how those situations are apt to progress. The following session illustrates how we can take impressions one step further, from being a simple piece of information to becoming a profound method of inner guidance.

1. **Stimulus:** Focus on a specific person or situation that requires higher guidance. Be sure that you are balanced and prepared to work with your intuition, and then ask Heaven for any information or guidance regarding the present circumstances.

Affirmation: "Heaven, allow me to be an instrument for your wisdom. Allow me to use my clairvoyant abilities to see the true nature of the situation and the best possible way to approach it."

2. **Response:** Again, after affirming your intention to work with your visual language, quiet your mind, then allow any impressions to flow in. Open yourself to any imagery that comes to mind.

3. **Synthesis:** When we ask for meaningful guidance through visual impressions, our answers often come in the form of metaphor. Not unlike a parable or poem, these visual metaphors often suggest a lesson by analogy or symbolism. Focus on becoming aware of the impression you are given, and then take it one step further by interpreting the image symbolically.

The following three case studies demonstrate how Heaven uses symbolic metaphor as a means of inner guidance.

CASE STUDY #1: Clairvoyant Information Through Metaphor

A woman is asked about the future of a specific couple's relationship by the male half of the couple. In response to this question, the woman receives an impression of a sunset, which gives her the feeling that "the sun may be setting" on this relationship. The general feeling around the image was calm and peaceful, so she tells the man that the two may have already had their day together, and that both may be prepared to move on to new horizons. The man responds that the pair had had a lifelong relationship, but that they had both been coming to the conclusion that they no longer had enough in common to stay together. A few months later, they amicably agree to go their separate ways.

CASE STUDY #2: Clairvoyant Guidance Through Metaphor

A man and a woman are having a conversation about the man's inability to solve a problem at work. Two of his employees are working, quite unsuccessfully, on two of his most important projects. As the man and woman discuss the issues, the thought of a man with his shoes on the wrong feet pops into her mind. She asks him, "What would you think if I told you that, in regard to this situation, you had your shoes on the wrong feet?" The man pauses, then says, "Well, there was some talk that I should have switched their projects—I think they each would have preferred to work on the other's project, but I felt differently." The woman suggests that maybe the man should consider matching the right foot with the right shoe. The man eventually agrees to do just that. Much to his satisfaction, productivity increases and the workplace becomes more rewarding.

CASE STUDY #3: Clairvoyant Information via Parallel Situations

A woman finds a lovely diamond and platinum ring in her mother's jewelry box. She picks it up and tries it on. As she wears it, she finds herself "remembering" a portrait she had once seen of her great-great-grandmother. Though she does not make the connection at the time, she is not surprised to later find out that the ring actually belonged to her great-great-grandmother.

As we have seen in this chapter, visual impressions (as well as all psychic impressions) can assist us in many ways, from the most mundane to the most profound. The more often we focus on clairvoyance, the easier it will become to understand the visual images and symbols that Heaven uses to communicate with us. Interpreting our visions is not unlike interpreting a painting or a photograph. Through clairvoyance, heavenly guidance is painted for us with imagery, symbols, metaphors, and analogies.

Clairaudience and the Word of Heaven

Clairaudient impressions can be either the most direct form of psychic impression or the most enigmatic. It is often hard to refute impressions that are given to us in the form of plain English, but, as with clairvoyant impressions, the subject matter can often be mysterious and require interpretation. As with clairvoyance, we often receive verbal impressions in the form of metaphor or parable. If Heaven paints us pictures with clairvoyance, it certainly writes us poetry with clairaudience.

The beauty about clairaudience is its propensity for interactive communication. Unlike clairvoyance and clairsentience, clairaudience naturally lends itself to two-way communication. When we are spoken to, we are inclined to speak back. So, it is possible for us to "converse" with Heaven. We can ask for clarification of our impressions; we can ask for more information; and we can respond, in the hopes that Heaven will likewise respond to us. Sometimes it does; sometimes it does not.

Clairaudient impressions are experienced as "thought language" more often than they are actually heard as "sound language." These thoughts may seem to have distinct voices or intonations, much as if we were remembering a person's voice. We can hear the voice in our head; we recognize the sound vibration and the speech patterns, but we do not actually hear anything. Other times, we may actually hear a voice or sound as loud and clear as if it occurred in the room with us. Either way, we normally experience clairaudience in our "mind's ear," and should not expect other people to hear what we do.

Session #1: Introduction to Receiving Clairaudient Impressions

In this session, we will focus on receiving impressions in our mind's ear via sound or language. These impressions will be focused on our lives and any guidance or validations that Heaven chooses to give us in that regard.

To begin the following session, take a few moments to prepare and balance yourself.

Suggestion: Meditate on the development of your capacity to hear your inner voice, and practice listening to your thoughts and the sounds that accompany them. Allow any sounds or words to flow with your stream of consciousness. Let stories unfold. Let music play through your mind as your thoughts unwind.

1. **Stimulus:** Ask for auditory intuitive impressions that you can confirm in your own life. Quietly center yourself and ask Heaven for general guidance or information surrounding your life at the moment. Do not focus on a particular question or specifics. Focus instead on receiving any information that may help you to understand your ability to communicate through clairaudience.

Affirmation: "I am an instrument of Heaven's highest wisdom. Allow me to strengthen my inner voice. Help me to listen. Allow me to hear."

2. **Response:** After affirming your intention to work with your clairaudient faculties, quiet your mind and then allow impressions to flow in. Open yourself to any random sounds, words, or music that enter your mind.

Remember: Listen without prejudice. Any phrases or melodies or noises that flow through your mind may be important pieces of information, once recognized.

3. **Synthesis:** Pay attention to the first impressions that you hear. Once you have become aware of the impression, try to focus on it. Notice if it becomes stronger, or if you become more certain of it the longer you focus on it. Sometimes songs will run as an endless loop through our minds. Sometimes words, names, or phrases will repeat themselves until we are conscious of them.

The following three case studies illustrate how certain individuals begin to recognize successful clairaudient impressions during the early stages of their psychic development.

CASE STUDY #1: Clairaudience and Music

A man wakes up in the morning with the melody and lyrics to a certain song running through his head. It is a song he has known for many years, but rarely hears. The melody loops in his head over a part of the chorus that contains the words "Everything is going to be fine, fine, fine . . . " He notices the song popping in and out of his head, throughout the day—a day that delivers bad news, including the termination of his position at work. Despite his anxiety and distress over potentially harrowing changes in his life, he feels that the song was Heaven's way of letting him know that the changes would be for the best.

CASE STUDY #2: The Voices in Our Head

A man is leaving for work in the morning. As he pulls out of his driveway, he hears the phrase "Better check the coffeepot" as if someone had just spoken it in his mind. The voice is very distinct, and is definitely a man's voice. Though the man decides to override his impression and continue on to work, he isn't at all surprised to find the coffeepot on fire when he returns home later that day. Fortunately, no major damage had occurred.

CASE STUDY #3: Clairaudeint Messages Through Mass Media

A woman is in the process of making an important decision about which company to hire for a specific project. She has a good offer from a company that she knows and likes, but an even better offer from a larger but unfamiliar company that promises more opportunity. As she is on the phone with her contact at the larger company, a slogan from a commercial she had heard earlier in the day pops into her head: "This is the one!" She decides to take a chance with the unfamiliar company, and winds up creating an excellent partnership that surpasses her expectations.

Each person will have a unique way of experiencing auditory impressions. It does not matter whether you hear the impressions with staggering clarity or within the subtlety of your mind's ear. As long as the message gets through, the process is successful.

Session #2: Seeking Guidance Through Internal Dialogue

With this session, we can practice recognizing our intuitive inspiration through inner dialogue. Undoubtedly we have all talked to ourselves without realizing the profundity of our conversations. Many times we are not just talking to ourselves; we are talking to our higher selves.

This process can be very enlightening and motivational. We simply open ourselves to our inner guidance, and then let the conversation flow back and forth, as in normal conversation. We can practice this during our meditations, during quiet moments in the car or shower, or whenever we are seeking advice for ourselves or others. There are three steps in this process:

1. **Ask a question:** Think "out loud" in your head as you ask your question.

Example: Ask yourself, "Am I prepared to take this next step in my life?"

2. **Receive a response:** Flow with the first response that comes to mind. This response may often address you in the second person, by your name, or even a pet name like "my child," or "my dear." The tone will most often be one of charitable understanding. (Any negative thoughts should be discarded, and the conversation ended.) Responses may be short and sweet or quite long and explanatory. Continue to go with the flow, and let the information flow as it comes.

Example: "You know the answer, my child. Y as long as you are prepared to follow your inner t yourself, and the rest will fall in line. With faith and courag thing is possible."

Most likely you will experience this as "thought," much as though you were talking to yourself. Do not expect to hear actual voices, though that may occur for some individuals. It may be difficult at first to be certain that you are experiencing anything other than your own thoughts. The content of the information that comes through will be the distinguishing factor in that regard. If you are receiving inspiring information that feels right, that supports your intuition and higher self on the path of truth, then you can be confident that you are tapping into your higher inner wisdom.

3. **Continue the dialogue:** Thinking to yourself, ask any further questions or present any other ideas that you might have.

Example:

Self: "But my heart is full of fear. I am afraid I will make the wrong choice, and not have the strength to carry it through."

Response: "No decision should be based on fear. If fear is a factor, then your decision is not coming from the light, but from darkness. All choices carry degrees of right and wrong; there is no absolute in this world. Choose the path that offers the highest good and you will not fail, even if you lack the strength. In time, it will come. Trust and be patient, my friend."

The dialogue should continue to roll as long as there is pertinent information to be expressed. You will know when it is time to stop. Consider writing down any important thoughts in your journal, for future reference. Inner dialogue work can help you to discover your true thoughts and feelings about the situations in your life, and also can help you navigate through them.

Clairsentience and Psychic Feelings

Our psychic feelings may be the most elusive and unpredictable of our intuitive experiences. When they do come, they are often the most convincing, and can move us like no other. Whether they touch us emotionally or physically, they are capable of moving us to a certainty of awareness and a deep level of understanding.

For the purposes of this section, the different types of psychic "sensations" are grouped together under the umbrella of physical and emotional responses to intuitive phenomena. Among others, these include emotional states; sensations or slight pains in specific body parts; tastes; and scents. Unlike clairvoyant or clairaudient impressions, which can be processed through a visual or literal language, these sensory experiences often have a dominant element of feeling, which serves as the driving force behind any meaning.

In Chapter 14 we will work with spirit touch, which also falls into this category of psychic feeling. Physical sensations of the spirit are not unlike spiritual sensations of our bodies. They are most often a direct result of our physical or emotional bodies interacting soul to soul, either with a soul in spirit or a soul incarnate. Either way, we are capable of touching in with each other with our soul energy, just as we would with our physical body. The following sessions are some potentially enjoyable ways that we can connect with other souls through our sense of feeling.

Session #1: Introduction to Receiving Clairsentient Impressions

In this session, we will focus on the ways in which we receive physical and emotional sensory information. We can "feel" information either physically or emotionally. We can absorb clairsentient energy from Heaven as information from our guides or other souls who have crossed over, but we can also absorb such energy from the people we come in close contact with. This is one reason it can be detrimental to live your life in a psychically "open" state.

To begin the following session, take a few moments to prepare and balance yourself. Take note of your present emotional and physical states, of any lingering feelings that may be afflicting your heart or your body. Once you have taken inventory, you can continue on with the awareness that any new physical or emotional sensations are likely to be sensory impressions from Heaven, not your own feelings.

Suggestion: Visualize your healthy and complete body and soul. Envision your body as a blank canvas. Any sensory impressions that follow will add their own color to this surface. These impressions will not be absorbed or accepted as your own, but instead viewed and understood objectively. Focus on feeling, then releasing. Feel the impression, understand the impression, and then let it go.

1. **Stimulus:** Ask to understand impressions using your psychic feeling. Quietly center yourself and ask Heaven to allow you to use your clairsentient abilities to gain insight into an appropriate situation. Clairsentient impressions most often give us information about the emotional and physiological states of another person or soul. This is the most common way to understand illness in the physical body, and also the cause of death for souls who have crossed over.

Affirmation: "I am an instrument of Divine wisdom. Allow me to strengthen and discern my psychic feelings. Allow me to feel."

2. **Response:** After affirming your intention to work with your clairsentient faculties, focus on the situation you are working with, switch into receiving mode, and then allow any impressions to flow in.

Remember: The sensations you feel are not your own. If a sensation ever becomes too intense or uncomfortable, ask that it be taken away. You then should notice the impression almost immediately pull back. Avoid carrying any sensory baggage with you after your sessions.

3. **Synthesis:** Pay attention to any feelings that arise. The slightest pains, tingles, or touches may be significant. Notice if your emotions are affected. Has your mood changed since you began the session? Do you feel tired? Angry? Sad? Overjoyed? Any shift in emotional state may be important information.

The following three case studies convey several ways that clairsentience can provide us with useful information.

CASE STUDY #1: Psychic Sensing Through Physical Feelings

The mother of a newborn baby notices that her child is getting a fever. The baby is fussy and troubled, but the mother does not know why. After scheduling a doctor's appointment, she holds her baby, and wonders what could be the problem. Soon, she begins to notice a dull ache in her left ear. The ache comes and goes on the way to the doctor's office, where they find out that the child has an ear infection in her left ear.

CASE STUDY #2: Psychic Sensing Through Emotion

A man is with his real estate agent, touring a prospective home. As he wanders through the house, he begins to feel sad, for no particular reason. The sadness soon progresses to distinct feelings of loss, so much so that he nearly is in tears. He cannot understand what has come over him, because he had felt fine earlier. By the end of the tour, the man learns that, just two weeks earlier, on Valentine's Day, the previous owner died unexpectedly of a heart attack, leaving behind a fiancé. The man takes a moment to mentally send the departed soul comfort and light, and soon the uncomfortable feeling within him subsides. He decides to buy the house, and lives there happily for many years.

CASE STUDY #3: Psychic Sensing Through a Sense of Knowing

A woman is driving home from a night class at her university. In the middle of her commute, she has a distinct feeling that something is wrong. She has no reason to feel this way, but nonetheless has an understanding that something around her is wrong. The next morning she learns that her grandmother had been rushed to the hospital the night before, and had nearly died at the exact time the woman had experienced her unexplained sensations.

Since they are so distinct, clairsentient impressions can be quiet unsettling if we do not understand them. People often react to strong feelings with fear because they do not understand what is happening to them. As we learn that these experiences are the way Heaven communicates information to us, we can accept the feelings with less fear and more proactive measures. Perhaps the grandmother wanted to let the young woman know as soon as possible that she was ill. Certainly, Heaven did not intend to scare her. Similarly, the man in the house touching in with the soul of the previous owner brought about understanding and awareness. There was no cause for fear.

Session #2: Clairsentience as a Means of Transcendental Experience

A most exhilarating and joyful way to experience psychic feeling is to open ourselves to the peace and comfort that Heaven perpetually offers. We do this naturally when we are feeling physically, spiritually, or emotionally uplifted, but we also can intentionally induce higher levels of consciousness or awareness. Through meditation, dance, yoga, and many other disciplines we relax and cleanse body and soul, so that we exist in a state more congruent with the divine.

1. **Raise your level of consciousness:** Take part in whatever spiritual practice allows you to balance your inner awareness and release yourself from daily distractions or anxieties. Meditate. Dance. Go walking in the woods. Free yourself from your earthly burdens; focus on a higher perspective.

2. **Open your self:** Ask that the love, beauty, joy, peace, goodness, and hope of the divine way be infiltrated into your being, so that you may feel it firsthand. As you elevate your state of being and open your soul to Heaven, you allow yourself to experience the divine peace of the moment. If you allow it, God's peace will soak into your soul, enriching and energizing you like the radiance and warmth of the sun on your skin on a cool winter day.

3. **Experience the inner calm of the moment:** From this higher perspective, feel the unconditional comfort that pervades even the most difficult situations in your life. Worldly issues become insignificant. We understand our hardships to be our lessons, just as our comforts are our blessings. Our hearts are filled with charity, and our souls brim with love. It is this love that is our home, which awaits our return. This love is all around us and within us. It is the eternal and the moment.

Regular practice of this sort of activity keeps us connected with our inner divinity and helps us to keep a higher perspective on our lives.

Psychic Senses Troubleshooting and Freq

The following are some common problems found the psychic senses:

Problem: "When I begin, my mind is a blank. I can't think of anything."

Explanation: This is the most common problem when beginning intuitive work. Our minds feel blank as we seem to grope for nonexistent information. Most often, the problem in this case is that we are thinking too much. The intuitive process is a receptive process, more than an active process. We do not need to go and get our information. When we relax, it will come to us.

Suggestion: Relax and trust. Let Heaven do the work.

Problem: "My mind keeps creating irrelevant or nonsensical images that get in my way."

Explanation: More often than not, these apparently nonsensical or irrelevant images are actually the impressions themselves. We mistake them for creations of our own mind because they are not what we are expecting. It is generally safe to say that when we are in our intuitive state, any thought that comes to mind is an intuitive impression. Don't make the mistake of disregarding images unless you are certain that your mind is interfering.

Suggestion: Suspend your judgment on impressions. Treat each thought as a potential impression, then see where it leads you. If more impressions begin to flow around it, then you will be glad you did not disregard it. If no other impressions follow, then carry on with the next thing that comes to mind.

Problem: "I can't tell the difference between my own thoughts and my intuition."

Explanation: Since impressions feel like our own thoughts, we may have a hard time knowing which information comes from Heaven and which information comes from our own mind. Time and practice will make the difference more clear.

Suggestion: Understand impressions on the terms listed below. This will enable you to better understand the way that genuine impressions feel. Remember, the truth will be found in the still point of quiet knowing, deep within ourselves, never in the din of our fears or the grasping of our wishes.

INTUITION VALIDITY TEST

We can apply this process to any intuitive information we receive:

- Do I have an emotional attachment to the information or its outcome?

If the answer is yes, then there is a good chance that your ego, or subjective personal emotions, could taint the process. To be true to your intuition, be true to God's will. Surrender your will to the will of Heaven, instead of basing it on what you think you want.

- How does the information feel?

You should feel calm and comfortable, at peace with your information. If you experience fear or anxiety, or notice yourself judging or being critical of a situation, then you can, again, suspect that your conscious mind is interfering with the process. Emotional or judgmental responses are characteristics of humanity, not of Heaven.

- How strong or repetitious is the information?

The stronger and clearer the information, the more likely it is to be genuine. Weak or vague information can be a result of our minds grasping for impressions, or formulating our own. Also, genuine information will often repeat itself and grow stronger the more that we focus on it.

Problem: "I get stuck. I seem to get a couple of good impressions, and then they stop and I don't get anymore."

Explanation: This can be a frustrating problem. You begin to get information, then find yourself hitting a wall. Most often this is a by-product of a kind of performance anxiety. We get so excited that the process is working that our minds kick into overdrive as we try to make sense of it all. That blocks the intuitive process. When we shift into action mode we close our receptivity mode, which shuts off the flow.

Solution: Allow the flow to continue by rolling with the information as it comes. Accept the information initially without doubt or judgment. Open yourself to the stream of consciousness; don't try to analyze or interpret until all information is received. As you gain more control over your ability you will be able to pause the flow when necessary, without severing it altogether.

Problem: "Sometimes I find myself receiving negative impressions, or impressions that do not seem to come from Heaven in a spirit of love."

Explanation: This kind of thing is not entirely unusual, and most often occurs when we are in an emotional or mental state that is off of our center. Our minds can interfere by bringing up our doubts or fears. The law of attraction also allows our unbalanced state of mind to attract random, but harmless, unbalanced energy in the ethers.

Solution: Meditate to rebalance your energy before continuing spirit work. Be as centered as possible when you open yourself intuitively. If a disturbing impression passes through your mind, ignore it. Do not dwell on it or give it any of your energy; simply let it pass by. Then move on to more positive thoughts.

Problem: "Sometimes the impressions I receive are just plain wrong."

Explanation: This is bound to happen to everyone during the process of intuitive development. It usually occurs more frequently in the early stages than at a professional level. But there are no guarantees, even at that point. Remember, this is a complicated human process with a margin of error, both in translation and interpretation. In order for the process to succeed, we must recognize the impressions from Heaven and also interpret those impressions correctly. This is an art that requires time and experience.

Solution: Focus on your success, rather than your failures. In this process, it is easy to get something wrong. Just remember that by all logical reason, it should be impossible to get something right through the intuitive process. Be patient. With experience, your accuracy will increase, as will your understanding of the reasons for your mistakes. "Misses" are usually just misunderstandings.

Summary

Now that you have completed this workshop, you should have a clearer idea as to which psychic senses come most naturally to you and which senses require more effort. Once you are aware of how the different meta-senses feel and function, you will notice that they often work together during the intuitive process.

Each of us will have our own style, or "psychic recipe," for receiving intuitive information. One person may be strongly clairvoyant, with a dash of clairsentience, and barely any clairaudience. Another person may receive nearly all impressions through the auditory faculties, with a regular peppering of visual symbols and physical sensations. One way of working is never superior to another, except in regard to the quality of information that is ultimately delivered.

Be comfortable with whatever process comes naturally to you. If you are naturally clairvoyant, focus on fine-tuning your visual perception and symbolic interpretations. If you are naturally clairaudient, develop your understanding of sound vibration, music, or language. If you are naturally clairsentient, learn to control your emotions and tap your strong feelings. Your range of experience will increase over time. Eventually, you may have all of your senses working in tandem, allowing you to be a most efficient instrument for communicating Heaven's word.

You don't have a soul. You are a Soul. You have a body.

—C. S. Lewis

Chapter 11

Your Body Is Your Temple: *Physiological Attunement and the Chakras*

When we develop a passion for spirituality, we may find it all too easy to live from our souls, to deny the importance of our physical nature. Souls are eternal. Bodies are temporary. We don't have to be Einstein to figure out which is the better place for our long-term investments. Nonetheless, if we deny our physical nature, we deny a very real and important aspect of ourselves. We are in physical form for a reason. And while we are here, our bodies can either assist our spiritual growth or hinder it.

The ideal state is for the body and soul to live in synchronicity. When this occurs, our intuition improves, our mind is clearer, and we feel more connected to the divine source. When body and soul are not in synchronicity, either mental or physical illness can result. When we understand our health holistically, we accept that, in many ways, the state of our bodies reflects the state of our souls. Illness is often a direct result of emotional or psychological blockages or distress. Illness is our cry for healing, on more than a physical level.

As we evolve spiritually, we may find it easier to cope with the aspects of our lives that were once a source of suffering and may have contributed to any ill health. Therefore, when we have healthier minds we will have healthier bodies. Conversely, when we take care of our bodies with proper diet and exercise, we create a more pure and energetic physiology, which in turn reinforces the purity and energy of our souls. Hence, we have healthier minds when we have healthier bodies.

There are many ways for us to use this symbiotic relationship to our advantage. We can begin by taking care of ourselves, both physically and spiritually. On the physical level, it is important to nourish ourselves sensibly, with proper amounts of sleep and exercise and a healthful diet. Sleep revitalizes our souls and allows our bodies to rest. Exercise strengthens our bodies and raises our energy levels. A proper diet nourishes our cells and may help to raise our body's rate of vibration. Vegetarian diets, in particular, are ideal for eliminating toxins and elevating energy levels.

Our physical health is largely determined by the way our bodies process energy. Material energy, such as air, water, or food, is processed through the internal organs and systems. Non-physical energy, such as thought and emotion, is processed through the body's energy field (the aura and chakras), which is electrically connected to our bodies via the nervous system. Our stomach flutters when we are in love. Our heart races when we are afraid. We blush when we are embarrassed. Every thought and emotion we have leaves its imprint upon the body, some in more noticeable ways than others. To understand how this works, we should familiarize ourselves with the body's chakra system.

The Chakras

Since ancient times, Eastern religion has taught us that we have a group of specific energy centers in our bodies called chakras. This term originates from the Sanskrit word meaning "wheel." Each center functions like a spinning vortex, or vast halo, channeling energy between our spiritual bodies and physical bodies. By connecting our physical bodies with the electromagnetic energy field that surrounds us, often referred to as the aura or spiritual life force, the chakras process emotions and thoughts as a form of energy. This energy can be vitalizing or it can be destructive, depending on our state of mind. Loving thoughts that stem from our higher selves provide our bodies with life-sustaining energy and healing. Fearful or negative thoughts often create blockages that prevent proper energy flow and set the stage for illness.

The locations of the primary chakras correspond to our bodies' main nerve ganglia, which emanate along the length of the spinal column. Their location reflects the intimate way in which they work with both our spiritual body, through our aura, and our physical body, through our nervous system. Each chakra serves as a sort of "transformer" in which high-frequency psychic energy activates our bodies. Each chakra is also associated with a specific color that reflects the type of energy it processes. The rainbow of the visual spectrum is represented, starting with the lower frequency reds and ranging to the highest frequency blues and violets.

The Major Chakras

1. First Chakra
   Area of the Body: Base of the spine
   Color: Red
   Focus: Material-world issues
   Balanced Expression: Safety, security, prosperity
   Imbalanced Expression: Fear, sloth, instability
2. Second Chakra
   Area of the Body: Abdomen and sexual organs
   Color: Orange

Focus: Desires
Balanced Expression: Creativity, sexuality, pleasure
Imbalanced Expression: Obsession, guilt, denial

3. **Third Chakra**
   Area of the Body: Solar plexus
   Color: Yellow
   Focus: Individual power
   Balanced Expression: Individuality, self-esteem, vitality
   Imbalanced Expression: Aggression, passivity, fearfulness, shame
4. **Fourth Chakra**
   Area of the Body: Heart center
   Color: Green
   Focus: Relationships
   Balanced Expression: Love, forgiveness, balance
   Imbalanced Expression: Jealousy, cynicism, co-dependence, grief
   This chakra unites the upper body and lower body energy centers.
5. **Fifth Chakra**
   Area of the Body: Throat
   Color: Blue
   Focus: Communication
   Balanced Expression: Self-expression, choices, resonance
   Imbalanced Expression: Lies, repression, harsh communication
6. **Sixth Chakra**
   Area of the Body: "Third-eye" point
   Color: Indigo
   Focus: Wisdom
   Balanced Expression: Self-awareness, clairvoyance, imagination
   Imbalanced Expression: Illusion, confusion, nightmares

7. **Seventh Chakra**
   Area of the Body: Crown of the head
   Color: Violet/White
   Focus: Spirituality
   Balanced Expression: Universal awareness, higher consciousness, bliss
   Imbalanced Expression: Attachment, skepticism, materialism

There are also minor, or tertiary, chakras that exist outside of the primary energy flow. These chakras correspond to different points throughout the body and serve to regulate the circulation of our vital forces. Tertiary chakras in the palms of our hands are associated with healing work. The practice of Reiki stimulates these centers, often producing sensations of heat or tingling in the palms. The lower tertiary chakras are located in our feet and knees, and serve to ground us to the earth. Minor chakras also are located behind our eyes and in many areas where we have heightened physical sensitivity.

The condition of both the major and minor chakras reflects our state of health, physically and spiritually. The balance or imbalance in a particular chakra is a manifestation of the balanced or imbalanced energy we put through it. All of our thoughts and experiences are filtered through these centers. When chakra energy is blocked by stress or other negative stimulus, emotional and physical illness can result. Once we understand the chakras, we may begin to work with them to enhance the healthy energy flow through our body and spirit.

Exercise

Exercise is a crucial factor in balancing our energy. The more we exercise, the more energy we have. When we engage in physical activity, our bodies become a conduit for energy flow. When we do not exercise, stagnant energies create blockages in our own energy flow. We then feel lethargic. We may experience backaches, headaches, and tension in different parts of our bodies. Regular exercise will help the body to flush out stagnant energy and renew the energy flow. Yoga, dance, sports, or even a walk in the park can refresh us and renew our energy supply.

Diet

Food has the capability of raising or lowering our body's vibration. A diet rich in "lighter" foods, such as fruits, vegetables, lean meats, and grains, provides the body with *clean* energy and sustains our bodies in an optimal manner. A diet rich in "denser" foods, like fast food, processed food, refined sugars, and stimulants such as caffeine or nicotine fuel the body with a polluted energy—the body will still run on it, but not optimally. Processed foods and beverages are harder to digest and provide fewer nutrients. In general, the closer our food is to its natural form, the better we will use its energy.

Most of us taking eating for granted. We do it so often that we rarely think about the profound nature of the digestive process. The physical material that we ingest is transformed into energy through digestion, as food molecules are broken down into particles small enough to be absorbed into the circulatory system. The circulatory system contains living cells, and is therefore alive. The vitamins and minerals we take into our bodies sustain this "river of life," which in turn sustains us and our energy levels.

Different people will have different comfort levels in regard to the types of food that provide optimal energy. Some individuals find that their bodies function best on vegetarian or vegan diets; others may stick to their eggs, unprocessed meats, and natural cheeses. Each of us must work with our own body chemistry to determine the types of foods that give us the purest energy and fuel for our life.

A healthful lifestyle, along with yoga, meditation, or any type of regular physical exercise, can assist us in freeing the energy flow in our bodies. As we evolve spiritually, and grow in our self-awareness, we find that our physical and spiritual bodies will begin to release blockages that we may have been holding on to for years. We facilitate this process by taking care of ourselves, by treating our bodies with respect. The body truly is a temple, for it is the home of the divine spirit within us all.

Wisdom is a sacred communion.

—Victor Hugo

CHAPTER 12

COMMUNION: *Vitalize Body, Mind, and Spirit by Connecting with the Divine Way*

The surest way to uplift our soul is to fill it with the heavenly spirit. God is within us, and all around us. The state of grace is pervasive, if only we will tap into it. Throughout history, human beings have discovered many ways of communing with the love and ecstasy of the higher powers. In tribal cultures, dance is ritualized in order to induce mystical experience. Saints, like St. Theresa, found heavenly raptures through prayer. Yogis lose themselves in transcendental yoga and meditation. All of these are examples of the ways human beings are drawn to experience the divine passion here on earth.

Experiencing this passion—communing with the divine spirit—reminds us of the divinity within ourselves and allows us to feel, even if only momentarily, the grace that the path of enlightenment promises. We uplift ourselves. We are revitalized. We feel our faith come to life. We raise our consciousness and find it easier to live from our higher selves, and to understand our intuition.

The following are just a few of the many ways available for us to experience, firsthand, the fulfillment of the heavenly spirit. These practices facilitate our spiritual growth and help us maintain the balance of body and spirit necessary for clear, intuitive understanding in our lives.

Meditation

When we meditate, we direct our attention within, centering ourselves through visualization and relaxation techniques in order to alter our state of consciousness. Meditation brings peace to our often chaotic lives and allows us to raise our vibrational level as we commune with Spirit and let go of worldly trifles. By doing so, we become more enlightened to the true meaning of our lives and become more aware of our inner guidance.

A common misconception about meditation is that it requires us to clear our minds of any thoughts. Realistically, our minds are often very full of activity during meditation. We may use our meditation time to visualize anything in our imagination: colors, symbols, places, activities. We may choose to focus on the rhythm of our breath in order to relax our bodies and dispel negativity. We may receive intuitive impressions or psychic messages. We may also interact with other spiritual beings during our meditations; we can get to know our spiritual families, connect with loved ones in spirit, and receive guidance from our teachers.

Meditation is an essential part of psychic development. We will learn that, through meditation, we are able to open ourselves to the depths of our inner power. By searching deep within ourselves, we can discover the spirit within—the ultimate mystery. We can use meditation to heal ourselves, to inspire our creativity, to explore higher realities, to cleanse our thoughts and emotions, or to find inner guidance. Meditation allows us to engage ourselves in a beautiful process of interior purification that leads to divine union.

By putting the conscious mind aside, we are, in essence, putting our "selves" aside. All of our judgments, inhibitions, and ego drives become less important. We can focus on receiving objective, selfless communion with the spiritual realm. A meditation routine helps us achieve this in two ways. First, it raises our energy level to a point at which our physical plane has greater potential for interaction with the higher spiritual plane. Second, it creates a safe and comfortable "place of mind" where we are free to receive information and impressions from our spiritual guardians. The more that we practice this routine, and take ourselves to this place, the more vivid our psychic understanding will become.

Meditation Workshop

There are several things you can do in advance to maximize your meditation experience.

Prepare for Meditation

- Establish a regular time of day for meditation. Build a routine.
- Save meals for after meditation. Digestion "grounds" us.
- Expect a duration of 20 to 30 minutes.
- Sit up as straight as possible, while still being comfortable.
- Do not try to make your mind blank or repress thoughts.

Gather Supplies

No supplies are *necessary* for meditation. We can meditate in the woods, or in a car, or in a box, if we have to. However, the following items can enhance the meditative experience and create an optimal environment for spirit work.

1. **A candle:** Lighting a candle is a metaphor for the process of illumination, as the element of fire transmutes physical energy into light. Lighting a candle prior to any type of spiritual work is both a symbolic and literal gesture of our dedication to God's light.

2. **A fresh bowl of water:** Water cleanses and absorbs energy, particularly any heavier energy in the air around us. Keeping a fresh bowl or glass of water in a room will help to neutralize unbalanced energy. It is important to change the water regularly, particularly once a significant amount of bubbles have accumulated on the container walls.

3. **Purification materials:** For thousands of years, the art of incense burning has been a crucial element of religious ceremonies and spiritual rituals throughout the world. Incense is known to purify our space, raise our vibrations, protect us from negative influences, and enhance healing. Incense fragrances, like frankincense and myrrh, are commonly used for their spiritually elevating influences. Sage, an herb that has been used for many years in Native American religious rituals, is often used for purification. This technique, called "smudging," allows us to purify body, mind, and spirit, as well as our living space and belongings. Burning incense or sage prior to or during your meditation can help to lighten the atmosphere around you, and uplift your spirits in the process.

Establish a Location and Prepare the Environment

It is preferable to designate a specific spot for meditation, perhaps a special chair, or bed, or even the bathroom, if that is the only place you can find privacy. Choose a place that is away from the traffic and energy flow of the general household. You will find the air clearer where there have been fewer disruptive energies.

Here are some simple tips for preparing your meditation environment:

- Go to your meditation spot during a time when you will not be interrupted.
- Turn off any extraneous electronic devices, such as televisions, dishwashers, and phones.
- Gather any pillows or blankets that will add comfort or relaxation.
- Turn on some light music, if you like. Preferably, it should be relaxing and instrumental.

Select a Position

There are many different body positions suitable for meditation. The ideal is to find a position that allows you to relax completely, yet without becoming so relaxed that you fall asleep. For this reason, lying down is not recommended. A preferable position would be a seated, upright position, in a comfortable chair or on a soft surface. It is important to find a position that will facilitate energy flow through your body. Do not cross your legs and arms. Your position should allow you to become fully relaxed. Once you are comfortable and settled, you can close your eyes and begin the following meditation exercise.

Inner Sanctuary Meditation

This is a quiet meditation to center the mind and dispel anxiety or fears. This meditation may help you to achieve the balanced state of awareness that is optimal for intuitive work. It is recommended that you do a brief exercise of this nature prior to any intense spiritual endeavors. The following meditation can be read and then repeated from memory, or read out loud to a tape recorder and played back for a guided meditation.

This exercise can be used any time that you need to center yourself. Regular spiritual communion like this will help to develop your ability to visualize and will strengthen your divine connection. Feel free to elaborate on or change the inner sanctuary that you create. Once you create it, go to it often. Get to know it, like a real place on earth, until it feels familiar. This will assist you farther down your road when you begin to work with your guides and seek guidance from the other beings in spirit who will meet with you thought to thought, mind to mind.

1. Begin with a series of deep, cleansing breaths. Breathe in to the count of four; breathe out to the count of four. Repeat slowly as you visualize a soothing white light, filled with peace and God's love flowing into you with every breath. Then visualize the release of all anxiety and fear with each exhalation.

2. Repeat until you feel a calm start to set in. Notice your body relaxing, your shoulders settling, your muscles releasing. Continue breathing this way for 5 to 20 more rounds. Chase away any worldly troubles by silently repeating to yourself: "All is God's will. I am an instrument of God's will." Once you have achieved a state of relaxation, continue with a natural, comfortable breathing pattern.

3. Now you are going to create a place where you are completely at ease and at peace. In this exercise, we are going to create a secret garden as our inner sanctuary. (In future meditations, you can envision any place you like, such as a tropical island, or an English meadow, or a mountaintop view—but choose a place that has meaning for you, maybe even a place that you have been to. It is best to create a place that is close to nature.)

4. Continue with a gentle rhythmic breathing as you begin to visualize a lush, sunlit forest. Streams of brilliant golden light beam down through the leaves and catch sparkles in the air. You notice that you're ascending a mountainside, on a soft path that has been worn into the earth. Higher and higher the path leads, and yet you do not grow tired. The air becomes lighter. Your feet seem to barely touch the ground. Your soul is uplifted and full of peace.

5. As you continue on, you notice that you are dressed in your favorite clothes. You feel vibrant, strong, and alive. You are at your best. The sun is warm on your face. Soon you reach a clearing atop the hill. The trees grow fewer until you can see two beautiful lilac trees creating an arched entrance to a garden. As you draw near, you are welcomed with the sweet scent of lilac from the blooming trees. Through the archway, you notice hints of color and beautiful foliage inviting you to come in. But you understand that you cannot enter until you leave all of your troubles behind. You reach down into the green grass at your feet and pick a dandelion seed head, the kind made for wishes. As you hold this soft white globe in front of your lips, you think of any worries or fears that you are still carrying with you at this time. Envision them becoming the tiny filaments of the flower, and then wish them away. Take a deep, cleansing breath, and gently blow all of the flower's filaments, along with your troubles, into the air. Watch them slowly disperse and disappear into the warm sunlight, to be taken by God's love.

6. You are now ready to enter the garden, this place of life, love, and peace. You may come here as often as you like, to meditate, to pray, or to visit with your friends in spirit. No one may enter your secret garden without an invitation from you. Today, you will get to know the garden. Look around you. What do you see? What kinds of flowers and trees surround you? What kind of ornamentation adorns the landscape? Fountains? Waterfalls? A babbling brook, perhaps? You certainly must find a comfortable

place to sit, maybe under a tall tree. Take a seat, and relax. Spend the next few minutes absorbing the beauty around you and letting the purity and love of this place circulate through your being.

7. Now, you feel calm and free from anxiety. You are completely comfortable in this place. This is your place, and it can be anything you want it to be. You thank God for this place, and for all of the goodness in your life and the world. Then you prepare to return home. As you exit through the archway, the lilac trees close over the entryway and bid you farewell with a shower of lilac petals as you begin to descend from the high hills. The sun is warm on your back. As the petals flicker and fall in the sunlight, all becomes light. The shimmering air becomes pure white and the forest fades behind it, until you are aware that you are at home, in your room, feeling refreshed and at peace. Open your eyes. Stretch. Smile.

Communication with God

Prayer is the key of Heaven.

—St. Augustine

It has been said that meditation is a time of listening to God, and prayer is a time for God to listen to us. In our prayers, we lift our hearts and minds to Heaven. We give thanks and affirm all of the good in our lives. We express reverence for our creator and appreciation of the beauty that the divine Spirit brings into the world. We ask for forgiveness, for clarity of mind, for peace of heart, for understanding and resolution of karma.

Prayer is a time for thanksgiving, for reparation, for adoration, and for petition. We can take this time to become consciously aware of our needs on spiritual, emotional, mental, and physical levels, and then express those needs. This is our time for spiritual dialogue. We ask questions. We receive answers. Many of the answers we seek can be found through the process of prayer.

Prayers

And so I say to you: Ask and you will receive; seek and you will find; Knock and the door will be opened to you. For everyone who asks will receive, and he who seeks will find, and the door will be opened to anyone who knocks.

—*Luke 11:9–13*

When we openly state our intentions or desires to the heavens, not only are we admitting our needs to and from God, but we are becoming more aware of our own needs in the process. Prayer can help us to understand and gain an awareness of our true purpose. When we adopt a genuine spirit of prayer, we become willing to surrender ourselves to the highest good, despite our subjective goals or ideals. Prayer allows us the opportunity to actively experience the mystery of divine grace.

Each individual will have affinities for different prayers based on their individual life paths. We may adopt any of the traditional prayers of world religions, or write our own, for our own specific paths. We may choose to memorize our prayers, or we may read them with good intention.

These are a few of the traditional prayers that can serve us well.

The Prayer of St. Francis

Lord, make me an instrument of thy peace,
that where there is hatred, I may bring love;
that where there is wrong, I may bring the spirit of forgiveness;
that where there is discord, I may bring harmony;
that where there is error, I may bring truth;
that where there is doubt, I may bring faith;
that where there is despair, I may bring hope,
that where there are shadows, I may bring light;

that where there is sadness, I may bring joy.
Lord, grant that I may seek rather to comfort than to be comforted;
to understand, than to be understood;
to love, than to be loved.
For it is by self-forgetting that one finds.
It is by forgiving that one is forgiven.
It is by dying that one awakens to Eternal Life.

Guardian Angel Prayer

Angel of God, My Guardian Dear
to whom God's love commits me here.
Ever this day be at my side
to light and guard and rule and guide.

Serenity Prayer

GOD, grant me the serenity
to accept the things
I cannot change,
Courage to change the
things I can, and the
wisdom to know the difference.
Living ONE DAY AT A TIME;
Enjoying one moment at a time;
Accepting hardship as the
pathway to peace.
Taking, as He did, this
sinful world as it is,
not as I would have it.
Trusting that He will make
all things right if I
surrender to His Will;

That I may be reasonably happy
in this life, and supremely
happy with Him forever in
the next. Amen

—Reinhold Neibuhr, 1926

Buddhist Prayer

May all beings be filled with joy and peace.
May all beings everywhere,
The strong and the weak,
The great and the small,
The mean and the powerful,
The short and the long,
The subtle and the gross:
May all beings everywhere,
Seen and unseen,
Dwelling far off or nearby,
Being or waiting to become:
May all be filled with lasting joy.
Let no one deceive another,
Let no one anywhere despise another,
Let no one out of anger or resentment
Wish suffering on anyone at all.
Just as a mother with her own life
Protects her child, her only child, from harm,
So within yourself let grow
A boundless love for all creatures.
Let your love flow outward through the universe,
To its height, its depth, its broad extent,
A limitless love, without hatred or enmity.
Then as you stand or walk,
Sit or lie down,

As long as you are awake,
Strive for this with a one-pointed mind;
Your life will bring heaven to earth.

Sutta Nipata

Mantras and Affirmations

It is mostly in recent years that the Western world has begun to embrace the mysterious capacity of the mantra to enhance physical and spiritual vitality. The mantra originated as a sacred utterance (syllable, word, or verse) that was considered to possess mystical or spiritual power. The word *mantra* literally means "that which protects (or frees) consciousness."

Mantras are repeated continuously for affirmation or sounded once with complete and deliberate focus. Repeating a mantra is, technically, a form of yoga. Its sound and thought vibrations activate the chakras and have the power to awaken our souls, as well as lead us to self-transcendence.

Though many cultures throughout human history have believed in the power of the spoken word, the specific use of the mantra dates back thousands of years to the Indian Vedic period. Shamans, monks, and religious ascetics have used the mantra as a tool to reach higher states of consciousness. In Western culture, we are embracing the mantra as a source of affirmation, to harmonize our body, mind, and soul. The repetition, or chanting, of a mantra unites our physical bodies with our spiritual intent. This is an invaluable tool for healing, for building self-confidence and success, for self-discipline, and for protection. A mantra can be used at any time, spoken out loud or repeated silently in the mind.

The subtle harmonic vibrations of chanted mantras, both mental and vocal, act as a cleansing and purifying agent for the consciousness. They protect us from the endless flow of thought, especially the thought that arises from our fears, negativity, or worry.

The subtle vitalizing frequencies of mantras activate psychic energies and awaken our intuitive faculties. They endow us with a propensity for divine rapture as we protect and encourage our souls.

We may use a mantra any time we feel that we need one. Create a phrase that addresses your intention—for strength, protection, peace, endurance, or whatever it is that you need at the time—and then repeat it, out loud or internally, over and over again. Notice how a positive affirmation uplifts us subtly, yet distinctly. The affirmation and the attention to positive thinking helps us to overcome the negative energy patterns that often consume our thoughts.

The following are examples of some simple phrases that we can employ as mantras or affirmations.

Centering Mantra

Peace is within me.
Calm. Peace. Balance.
All will be well.
Om shanti (I am peace).

Intuitive Development Mantra

I am a clear channel.
I am open to my higher self.
Heaven speak through me.

Protection Mantra

I surround myself with the peace of Christ.
God's love and light protect me.
The Lord is my shepherd.

Single Phrase Mantra

Ohm, I am, Love, Peace, God, Light, Faith.

As we repeat the chosen word or words, we may initially contemplate the meaning, but ultimately we lose ourselves in the rhythmic stillness of repetition. Deep, cleansing breaths should accompany the mental or verbal repetition, thus uniting body and mind in the centering process. The mantra becomes a symbol for our intention, our aspiration. The more that we affirm it to ourselves, the more it comes alive in our life.

Yoga: Holistic Healing for Body and Spirit

If I'm losing balance in a pose, I stretch higher and God reaches down to steady me. It works every time, and not just in yoga.

—*Bella Convalesco*

Yoga, as well as many other forms of physical activity, is beneficial for keeping our body energy and soul energy balanced. This ancient practice holistically strengthens and restores our body, mind, and spirit. On the physical level, yoga tones muscle, massages the internal organs, and reinforces proper spinal alignment. The relaxation and breathing techniques relieve stress and lower blood pressure. On a psychological level, yoga refreshes our minds, improves our concentration, and can improve our general mental state.

Regular practice of yoga can alleviate blockages in the chakras and assist the body with processing and eliminating any damaging psychic energy or attitudes. The postures of the body during a yoga session are formulated to stimulate the conduits of the psychic channels, or Nadis, which connect to our nervous system and conduct our life force throughout the body. Thus, by practicing yoga regularly, we positively influence both our physical and spiritual well-being.

Music: Experiencing God Through Sound

Music is well said to be the speech of angels.

—Thomas Carlyle

Whether we are creating it or appreciating it, music has the power to move our souls. The aesthetic emotion that is roused by music has the ability to elevate, energize, and nourish our being. Music uplifts us. It excites us. It comforts us. It unifies us. It enables us to transcend our individual consciousness and to experience the ecstatic union of the soul.

For this reason, music has been an essential part of nearly all types of religious ceremonies throughout human history. Singing, dancing, and playing musical instruments serve to assist us in raising our spirits during worship or any kind of celebration. When we elevate ourselves in this way, we are able to connect with ourselves on a higher level. Musical vibrations harmonize with our own energy and unite us with the world beyond our individual selves. When we are moved deeply by music, we temporarily lose the illusion of separateness that is part of the human experience. When we experience the music, we become part of it, and part of something that is more than ourselves.

This is the state where our inner guidance functions at its peak. Here, we are free. Here, we rise above the din of our worries, and find clear answers in our life. But music does more than affect our emotional and spiritual bodies; it also can have a profound impact on our physical well-being. Sound therapy is becoming popular in Western culture, and it is theorized that sound waves actually activate healing on a cellular level. Recent medical research has suggested that sonic frequencies appear to interact with our cellular vibrational levels, and assist in maintaining a healthy resonant frequency in our bodies. In this way, music enriches the quality of our lives, while also stimulating our soul's awareness.

Dance

Dance meditation approaches dance as a meditation and meditation as a dance. Both are an entwined opportunity to explore the relationships between self-&-other, self-&-cosmos, self-with-self and self-to-The Divine Eternal . . . it fosters the recognition of our inherent ability to heal and self-regulate. It assumes and enhances an abundant body-mind integration. It encourages receptivity, creativity and present-ness.

—Dunya Dianne McPherson

When we are moved by music, we are moved to dance. Our bodies move physically as our souls are moved ethereally. The raptures and ecstasy of dance, and the transcendental states that can accompany it, range from the most passionately instinctual to the most spiritually elating.

In this world, there are few ways to commune with the divine that are as intense as dance. Spiritual dancing has permeated cultures across the globe since the dawn of time. Tribal dancing and shamanic rituals have inspired visions and healings as the dancer experiences the divine ecstasy of spiritual wholeness. When we dance, we lose ourselves. We become one with the spirit that moves within us, one with the moment in which we exist.

When we dance, we experience greater insights into the truth of our own existence. Dance can open doorways to levels of higher consciousness which are characteristic of states of trance or ecstasy. Dance stimulates the imagination and, therefore, cultivates our intuitive readiness. In this regard, dance functions as a sort of "active" meditation. We regulate our breathing, we raise our vibrations, and we purge ourselves as new, vital energy flows through our spirit.

Spiritual dancing allows us to be one with the moment, to surrender our worldly anxieties and live in the eternal present. We experience ourselves fully, as body, mind, and soul actively unite in divine communion. We elevate ourselves. We become more fully alive.

While most of the practices described in this chapter are not essential for intuitive development, they will certainly help us to create a lifestyle that is conducive to the growth of new levels of spiritual awareness. We do not need to pray or meditate every time we need assistance in our lives, but we may want to if we are feeling too unbalanced to make our decisions clearly. We will have to learn to live from our higher selves no matter where we are, or what we are doing, whether we are in the quiet of our own homes, or lost in a crowd of worldly distractions. When we take the time to nourish our being in spiritual communion, we allow the heavenly Spirit to live within us, and create a lifestyle in which we are more open to higher awareness.

A perception, sudden as blinking, that subject and object are one, will lead to a deeply mysterious understanding; and by this understanding you will awaken to the truth.

—Huang Po

CHAPTER 13

PSYCHIC RECEPTIVITY: *Controlling Our Inner Power*

As we begin to open ourselves up to the more subtle dimensions of our reality, our boundaries will be tested. We will begin to experience things that we may or may not choose to accept. Our imagination will push the limits of our intellect. Is this real? Am I imagining this? These are the most common questions that we ask ourselves as we begin to work with the spiritual realm.

There are three general approaches that we may take as we process spiritual possibilities:

- the unwavering skeptic
- the unwavering believer
- the skeptical believer

The unwavering skeptics are the people who refuse to acknowledge any kind of phenomenon that cannot be explained through rational understanding. These are the people who would take a gun to an exorcism, and who look for their answers within the established laws of physics. Coincidences, for them, are usually meaningless. The unseen forces are irrelevant, if they exist at all.

The unwavering believers are at the other extreme position. These are the people who will believe *anything* that they think justifies their beliefs. These people often abandon intellectual function altogether as they desperately seek their truth. For them, *everything* is a sign; *everything* has a meaning that suits their agenda.

There may be distinct psychological motivations for each of these approaches to life, but such drastically opposing viewpoints often fuel the stereotypes that surround spiritual living.

The intellectual believers have the most sensible, balanced approach. As oxymoronic as it may sound, it is the consent of our reason that propels us into true belief. In this regard, it is important to be aware of the difference between our intellect and fear-based doubt. Doubt that is based on fear calls us to abandon our truths for fear of their consequences. Fear-based doubt makes us slaves. On the other hand, our reasonable doubt, or intellect, is not based on fear, but on the deductions made from our human experiences. Our intellect integrates new ideas into our understanding. This is an important faculty that grounds us, and allows us to maintain sobriety amidst the rapture of the spiritual experience. Following our intuition does not suggest the abandonment of our intellectual functions.

Intuitive Development Meditation

This meditation is designed to foster our intuitive abilities and encourage us to open ourselves consciously to the spiritual realm. This meditation is an excellent way to symbolically open ourselves to our spiritual potential. We may create many variations of this kind of meditation. Our intuition will guide us, as it does at any other time. Our higher selves will always know what we need, usually before our conscious minds do.

1. Begin with a series of deep, cleansing breaths. Breathe in to the count of four; breathe out to the count of four. Repeat slowly as you visualize the white light of peace and God's love flowing into you with every breath. Visualize the release of all anxiety and fear with each exhalation. Repeat until you feel a calm start to set in. Notice your body relaxing, your shoulders settling, your muscles releasing. Continue breathing this way for 5 to 20 more rounds. Chase away any worldly troubles by silently repeating to yourself: "All is God's will. I am an instrument of God's will." Once you have achieved a state of relaxation, continue with a natural, comfortable breathing pattern.

2. Now, return to your inner sanctuary, the one you created in Chapter 12. Take your time. Go through your entrance ritual. When you have reacquainted yourself with this place, pause and relax.

3. On the ground before you, you now notice a beautiful purple cloth. In the middle of the cloth you see a tall white candle; a vase of mixed roses, budded but not yet in bloom; and a bowl of water. Light the candle. Understand that your lighting of this candle is bringing a new light into your intuitive mind, creating light where there was darkness. Your intuition and spiritual growth are ignited like the wick of the candle. As this candle provides light and warmth, so will the knowledge you gain from feeding the fire of your own intuition. Next, look at the roses and notice that the small, multicolored buds are slowly turning toward the light and opening into bloom. As their petals slowly unfurl, you join them, bathing in the light and opening yourself to the spiritual warmth that surrounds you. Like the flowers, your intuition blooms when it is fed by the divine light.

4. Finally, pick up the container of water. Notice how cool and crystal clear this water is. Then notice the sound of water from

a nearby stream. Stand up and follow the sound until you reach this stream, carrying your vessel of water. When you arrive, you are in awe of the purity and beauty of this body of water. It looks refreshing and clear, just like the water in the container you are holding. Slowly descend the banks of the stream, wading deeper and deeper into the gentle waters. First the waters hug your ankles, then your knees, then your hips, and finally your chest. You lower your bowl of water into the stream and watch the two bodies of water become one, as the vast current of the stream flows into your vessel and absorbs the water that was previously yours. You understand that these are the holy and healing waters of the Spirit. As they take you in, you feel your feet lift off the bottom until you are floating gently downstream. You feel safe and relaxed because you know that you are in God's hands. Feel the flow all around you. You go wherever the flow takes you. Feel at one with the water, and enjoy the beautiful journey through nature.

5. Continue on as you like, floating, swimming, bathing, or wading, whatever you enjoy. Know that by joining the water, you are becoming part of the eternal flow of Spirit. Allow that stream to flow through your being, so that you may express the love and goodness of God to the world.

6. Soon, you will realize that the stream has brought you back to the same place where you entered. You climb up the riverbank, feeling alive and rejuvenated. As you return to your favorite place, you thank God for filling your heart with so much joy and life. It is time, now, to go home. The purple cloth is again before you. You blow out your candle, then watch the roses close back up into their buds. There they will remain until the next time you choose to visit this place. Exit as before, through the archway. The lilac trees close behind you and bid you farewell with a shower of petals as you begin to descend from the high hills. The sun is warm on your back. The shimmering air becomes pure white and the forest fades behind it, until you are aware that you are back in

your room, feeling refreshed and at peace. Open your eyes. Stretch. Smile.

Controlling Intuition

In order to maintain proper control over our intuitive abilities, we should be able to turn them on, or shut them off, according to our own will. It is up to us to control our conscious minds in a way that prevents us from being bombarded with unsolicited psychic information. If we have disciplined ourselves, we will for the most part be able to control when we want to interact with the spirit realm, and when we do not.

Realistically, most of us who are just beginning to tap into our intuitive energy generate enough mental static with everyday thoughts to eliminate the problem of receiving too much psychic information; we may be lucky to get *any* psychic information at first. In essence, our moment-to-moment thoughts create a barrier that blocks out more subtle, intuitive energy. When we quiet these thoughts, and focus inward, we allow the more subtle energies to have a voice. The more we focus on this voice, the louder it will grow. Therefore, it is essential for us to establish proper intuitive habits for the day when our unmitigated success arrives.

When we are planning to work with our intuition, we can create a brief ritual to open up our minds to our higher selves and the spirit realm. Then, when we have finished our intuitive work, we can end with a brief visualization of closing our psychic centers. It is not healthy for most people to remain open to the higher energies all of the time. Allowing this to happen puts us in danger of absorbing too much energy, or energy that does not belong to us. Either situation can negatively affect our state of being. We always want to be intuitive and "sensitive" in our daily lives; nonetheless, we do not want to become oversensitive in a way that keeps us from maintaining our inner balance.

Turning On Psychic Reception

Quiet your mind. Center your thoughts. Take several deep, cleansing breaths. Then visualize any one of the following while focusing on opening your mind to your higher self.

Opening a Gate or Door

Unlatch or unlock the gate or door and open it. Envision the other side of the threshold showering you with light and wisdom. Affirm that you are prepared to temporarily "open" yourself to information from the divine source. You are only open to that information which comes from the best and the brightest, in the spirit of truth and soul evolution.

Turning On a Switch

This switch, or lever, may illuminate a room, or turn on a screen where you may visually receive information. Affirm that you are now "turning on" your psychic receivers, and that you will only accept information from the best and the brightest, in the spirit of truth and soul evolution.

Blooming Flower

Imagine a beautiful flower, turning to the light and opening into full bloom. Affirm that the heavenly light and wisdom feeds your soul and guides you to the divine spirit. You will only absorb that information which comes from the best and the brightest, in the spirit of truth and soul evolution.

Turning Off Psychic Reception

Again, quiet your mind. Center your thoughts. Take several deep, cleansing breaths. Then visualize one of the following while concentrating on grounding yourself and stepping out of your intuitive zone.

Closing a Gate or Door

Close the gate or door and latch or lock it, while reminding yourself that you will return at another time to continue your work.

Turning Off a Switch

Move the switch or lever to a temporarily "off" position, reminding yourself that though you will keep the light in your heart, you will not work with it directly again until you return on another day.

Retreating Flower

Many plants will close their blooms or leaves at night. In the same way, we want to close our sensitivity during our daily life. Visualize the petals of a flower closing gently over you, protecting your sensitive inner core from unsolicited psychic impressions.

Grounding

After we spend any significant amount of time working with the spiritual realm, we may find ourselves on a natural "high." Working with psychic energy feels good. The energy that connects with us often uplifts us naturally, as the good vibrations flow through us. While this is a positive, pleasurable experience, after a period of such work we may feel the need to reground ourselves—to come back down, so to speak. The most common way to do this is to have a meal. Eating engages the body's digestive system, ultimately returning the body's vibrational level back to normal. Some people also find that a quick nap or physical exercise will reset the body's energy level. It is important to find a way to comfortably reintegrate into our daily routines. Not grounding ourselves properly can cause us to deplete our energy levels and can ultimately cause fatigue or stress.

When we work with our psychic energy responsibly, we can open ourselves to very emotionally, spiritually, and physically rewarding experiences. The key is to find the best process for our individual needs, then stick with it. In time, we will have a better understanding of our boundaries and energy levels, and so be the best intuitives that we can be.

Belief consists in accepting the affirmations of the soul;
Unbelief, in denying them.

—Ralph Waldo Emerson

CHAPTER 14

EXPLORING INTUITION: *Working with Our Higher Guidance*

Genuine psychic development should manifest as a by-product of soul evolution. Our intuition, as well as metaphysical experience in general, carries with it a great responsibility. We must handle our spirits with care. We must use our personal power in service to the higher truth. If we make the mistake of serving a lesser truth, such as our egos, or even the egos of others, we risk distorting eternal truth, and deluding ourselves in the process. We will function best in any intuitive capacity if we strive to be *psychic* insofar as we are also *spiritual.*

The process of intuitive and spiritual understanding may take many years, depending on our individual readiness. There may be times when our lives are receptive to this new growth. There also may be times when we are busy living, times when we feel that we are not growing at all. But sometimes the moments of slow growth are our greatest lessons. Our trials bring us the deepest spiritual understanding; it is only when we face our selves, our deepest fears, and our deepest aspirations that we will find true spiritual enlightenment.

If we commit ourselves to our spiritual development, it will come. It is only a matter of time, dedication, and a little bit of patience. Nonetheless, there are ways to reinforce our intentions and assist our higher selves with this developmental process. Manifestation is the process by which thought becomes reality. When we invest our energy into our intentions, we invest in the manifestation of our dream. We can apply this process to any kind of growth, particularly spiritual growth. By envisioning our success, we align ourselves consciously with our desired outcome.

Awareness of Our Spiritual Family

We can begin our inner journey by becoming more aware of the unseen energies and beings that populate our lives. When we have reason to believe that we actually do have guides and loved ones with us day to day, we will be able to feel a new level of support and comfort in all we do.

It can be very rewarding to establish a more conscious relationship with a spirit guide or "guardian angel." Though this is not necessary, because our guardians will take care of us whether we are aware of them or not, the process helps us to begin to understand the *personal* nature of the spirit world. Our experiences are not with vacant energy forms or vast, nebulous forces. They are the by-products of our interactions with a spiritual world filled with beautiful, individual beings. To gain more awareness about these beings, we need only look within ourselves. We are able to gain insight into the nature of these souls, their personalities, their names, their history with us—all through our intuition. It can be very rewarding to establish a more conscious relationship with a spirit guide or "guardian angel."

The following meditation can create an environment for

our spirit friends to reveal themselves to us, if the time for that is right.

Meeting Your Spiritual Family Meditation

1. Begin with a series of deep, cleansing breaths. Breathe in to the count of four; breathe out to the count of four. Repeat slowly as you visualize the white light of peace and God's love flowing into you with every breath. Then visualize the release of all apprehension with each exhalation. Repeat until you feel a calm start to set in. Notice your body relaxing, your shoulders settling, your muscles releasing. Continue breathing this way for 5 to 20 more rounds.

2. Affirm your intention to begin to consciously assist your spiritual guardians. Ask that, if the time is right in your spiritual evolution, that your personal guide be present, and come to you during the meditation.

3. Quiet your mind once more, then return to your inner sanctuary, which should be a comfortable place for you by now. Take your time. Go through your entrance ritual. When you have reacquainted yourself with this place, be still.

4. Tell your guide that it is time for him or her to join you in your sanctuary. Reaffirm that your guide has permission to enter this sacred place with you, and then let your mind go. Relax. Be aware of any presence you may feel with you in this inner sanctuary, in your "imagination."

5. Do not be surprised if you quickly begin to "imagine" a person with you, or greeting you. This most likely is not your imagination at all, but your mind's imaginative response to the impressions your spirit guide is giving you. Pay attention to any details—physical appearance, personality, age, and so on—as well as any dialogue that is initiated. You may well feel that you

imagine someone meeting you with a warm hug, or a handshake, or joking with you, or greeting you in any number of ways; go with your "imagination," even though it may feel awkward at first.

6. Suspend any disbelief, at least long enough to get a feel for how you are visualizing this individual. You may ask any questions or initiate any sort of conversation. Reaffirm that this is *your* place of learning, and that all information that passes through it must be in the divine spirit. Continue your interaction with this individual for as long as you like, and then express your intention to return to your normal state of consciousness. Bid your farewells, then exit as usual, through the archway; the lilac trees close behind you as you descend from the high hills. The sun is warm on your back. The shimmering air becomes pure white and the forest fades behind it, until you are aware that you are back in your room, feeling refreshed and at peace. Open your eyes. Stretch. Smile.

As we record our impressions over time, we may start to notice patterns and consistencies that we would have otherwise overlooked. If we begin to "imagine" the same individual coming to us during meditation, we can get to know this being and become more confident that he or she is more than a figment of our imagination. Truth takes time. We should not expect to receive it overnight.

Each person will have a unique experience when they initiate contact with spiritual friends in this way. There is no right or wrong experience. If no one showed up, we may have been too distracted, or we may not yet be ready for this step. If we are still harboring fears about the process, or laboring under false conceptions about our motives, our efforts may be blocked until we have changed our level of awareness. We are free to try again at another time, when we are certain we are centered and open.

Whether the information we receive from this kind of meditation is nebulous or most profound, it is important to make note of our impressions for future reference. Journal-keeping is also recommended throughout this process. Our memory alone will omit many important details that may only be captured by recording our experiences immediately after they occur. Also, we may not understand many of our experiences until a much later time, and may need to refer back to previous events for validation.

Spirit Touch

When our soul friends are among us, they may often make us aware of their presence with subtle physical sensations. Spiritual energy can be felt in many different ways, and is usually different for every person. It can be felt as a tingling sensation, or warmth, or powerful currents running through our bodies, or any of these things together. These impressions may be so subtle that we do not recognize them. On the other hand, they may be all-consuming, particularly if the spirit world is intent on getting our attention.

The best time to become aware of clairsentient spirit touch is during meditation. At this time, our body is relaxed and we are in a position to notice any extraordinary physical sensations. When we are in this quiet state, it is not unusual to feel subtle sensations or changes in our physiology. These sensations may feel electric in nature, or like a tingling on our skin; they are often similar to the energy we feel during a Reiki treatment. When we are "touched" by a spirit, we are usually experiencing a spirit's energy interfacing with our body's electromagnetic energy.

The most common places to feel this touch are in the region of the third eye (the forehead region), around our eyes, and on the tips of our noses, though we may feel it anywhere in the body. The sensations may come and go. It will feel as though it originates from an outside source, and will be distinct enough to be distinguished from our imagination. The touch is usually not so much a physical touch as it is an energy touch, but we feel it distinctly as it transmits through our nervous system.

It is possible to consciously solicit this kind of sensation as a means of communication with our friends in spirit. We can understand this as a way for them to make us aware of their presence, once we have learned to perceive their touch. Different souls may touch us in different ways or different locations, in order to identify themselves. Reiki and other forms of energy work may increase our sensitivity to spirit touch.

Spirit Touch Meditation

1. Sit quietly during your meditation. You may want to go to your inner sanctuary, to create a peaceful state of mind. When your mind has quieted and you are relaxed, ask to become aware of the touch of your closest spiritual guardian.

2. Be still and notice any distinct or subtle sensations on or around your body. You might feel as though there is a hair tickling against your face, when there is no hair to be found. You might feel something as slight as a light tingling sensation on your skin, or something as intense as a pouring rush of energy surge over you. You might feel a tickle on your nose. Each person will have a unique way of sensing energy. No matter what you are feeling, you should never feel anything painful or overwhelming. If this should ever be the case, stop your activity at once. Be still and notice any distinct or subtle sensations on or around your body.

3. When you notice a sensation, but are not necessarily sure that it is the touch of spirit, as opposed to your own imagination, ask that the sensation be repeated. For validation, souls may touch us at our will, at least initially, until we can attribute the specific sensation to the soul who is creating it.

We should pay close attention to the intuitive impressions we receive as we feel spiritual energy in our bodies. This will help us to understand who is with us at the crucial moments in our lives. If we cannot feel anything at first, our ability to feel and work with the energy consciously will grow as our meditation skills improve and our overall sensitivity increases. Once we do become aware of spirit touch, we can recognize it as a meaningful validation of the presence of our spiritual companions.

Inspirational Writing

Everything leads us to believe that there is a certain state of mind from which life and death, the real and the imaginary, past and future, the communicable and the incommunicable, height and depth are no longer perceived as contradictory.

—*André Breton,* Second Manifesto of Surrealism *(1929)*

The stream of consciousness that flows through palm and pen can carry us on a beautiful journey. Poets and writers have long known the beauty and truth that illuminate our inspirational hours. In the moments when the words come together with a life of their own, when the story writes itself, the spirit speaks through us. We are the instruments. Language is our medium.

The idea that we can access superconscious information through writing is not a new one. Inspirational writing has been influential in psychology and parapsychology as well as the arts, specifically in the surrealist movement. This kind of writing embraces the absence of all critical intervention during the creative process. We let the words flow, much as we allow our intuition to flow, without judgment and without attachment to the outcome. It is not surprising that surrealist writers sometimes refer to themselves as "medium-poets"; the idea of the medium-poet unifies the creative and metaphysical processes. A medium stands on the threshold between material and spiritual reality.

The mediumistic process, which functions through intuitive thinking, speaking, or writing, transcends the boundaries of the two worlds. Much can be accomplished when the material unites with the spiritual, and when creativity unites with intuition.

Whether we are writing for beauty or writing for truth, there are many techniques that we can employ to use inspirational writing in our own lives. Many poems, songs, essays, manifestoes, and even novels have been written via inspirational writing. When we write inspirationally, automatically, we open to our higher selves, who can access all levels of knowledge and wisdom. When we let go, and allow our inspiration to take over, we shift our awareness in a way that helps us achieve an expanded state of consciousness. In some cases, this expansion is so great that the writer enters into a trance state.

 Inspirational Writing Workshop

Getting in Touch with the Higher Self Through Writing

The following are examples of specific ways we can use inspirational writing regularly in our lives to connect to the divine source and enhance both our creativity and intuition. We can also utilize the process to access specific kinds of information or guidance from our higher selves. This is an excellent process for self-discovery, for understanding both our past and present lives.

Tips for Inspirational Writing

The following suggestions may help you to understand how to use writing to get in touch with your higher self:

- Go with the flow. Begin to write, then free-associate. Let whatever comes into your mind flow to the paper.
- Analyze nothing you receive until you put your pen down.
- Modify any of the following sessions to your own subject matter or interests.
- Keep in mind that any information you receive is still subject to your critical and intuitive judgment after delivery. You always have free will to accept or reject anything you experience. No process should make your decisions for you.
- If you are uneasy with any information that you are receiving, discontinue and return to the process another time. Your fears or anxieties may be interfering with the process.
- You may adapt any of these sessions to the process of inspirational *speaking*, using a tape recorder instead of a journal. Some people find that they are more inclined to either writing or speaking. You should embrace whichever process functions best for you.

Preparation for Inspirational Writing

Choose a quiet time and place to write, a time when you are feeling centered; if you like, briefly meditate and ask for divine guidance and inspiration during your writing sessions.

1. Gather paper, preferably a journal in which you can archive your information, and a pen that writes easily. You can also use a computer and keyboard if you prefer.
2. Settle into a comfortable writing position, in a place where you will not be disturbed.
3. Decide what information you would like to work with. Write this down at the top of the page. If you have a specific question, write it down, then open your mind to objective answers.

4. Affirm that you will only accept information and guidance in the divine spirit of wisdom, and that you are an instrument of Heaven.

Receiving Inner Guidance Through Writing

It is often difficult to see truth through the fog of our subjective emotions. Inspirational writing can be the perfect forum to work through our life issues by communicating with our higher self, or spirit guides.

1. **Stimulus:** Begin, as usual, by focusing on a specific situation that you are dealing with in your life. Write down your question, or simply start to journal your feelings about the choices you are making.
2. **Response:** Allow any guidance to flow. As you continue to write, you should begin to notice bits of guidance and perspective slipping into the text. You may actually begin to write in a style that refers to you in the second person. Continue to write until you feel that the flow has run its course.
3. **Synthesis:** Take a moment to clear your mind, and then go back and reread the information you just transcribed. Take note of the guidance you receive, and how it may improve your awareness. Notice how you feel about the information, and if your intuition is comfortable with it. You can also bring any of these ideas into your meditation to further work through them.

CASE STUDY #1: Inspirational Writing as a Means of Problem Solving

1. **Stimulus:** A man is seeking guidance as to whether or not he should take a chance on a new creative venture.

He asks Heaven to help him understand the higher nature of his choice.

2. **Response:** To initiate the flow, he begins writing about his uncertainties and hopes. He is afraid of losing the security of his current situation, but understands that he has the potential for more fulfillment if he accepts this opportunity. As he continues to write, words and guidance begin to flow freely, so much so that he can hardly keep up with them with his pen. The following is an excerpt from his journal: "Your life has been a constant tug of war between your sense of responsibility and your desire for freedom. Make the choices that you can live with. Make the choices that are best for your soul, not the ones that are easiest. There are no guarantees in life; there is no security, for the long run, for any choice. There are only choices that will propel our lives closer to or further from self-actualization."
3. **Synthesis:** The man can understand how this direct form of guidance applies to the larger themes he has been struggling with his entire life.

CASE STUDY #2: Writing as a Means of Emotional Understanding

1. **Stimulus:** A woman is very upset that her only son has decided to go to college in another city. She cannot understand why he would want to move away from his family, and hopes to find some understanding.
2. **Response:** To initiate the flow, she makes note of the issues with the situation. As she continues to write, a sense of comfort and acceptance begins to settle into her mind as the following words flow through her: "His decisions on how to live his life are not a direct reflection of his love for you. We come into this life with purpose

and karma to resolve. If he is called to another place, be sure there is a reason for it. You mustn't interfere with his life purpose. Part of your life purpose is to become your own center; this is just one situation which will test and hopefully enable your ability to live your life for yourself, instead of for pleasing those around you."

3. **Synthesis:** In this case, the woman's experience was accompanied by a clairsentient impression. The feeling of calm she felt was no doubt part of Heaven's consolation to her. As she opened herself up to higher understanding, she was able to grasp the larger picture of the situation, instead of clinging to her fears and perceived needs.

Connecting with Our Spiritual Family Through Writing

Through the process of inspirational writing, we can learn about the characteristics of our spiritual companions/teachers or even communicate with loved ones who have already passed on. This process is commonly referred to as channeling. We allow information from specific individuals in spirit to come to us and through us. Experiences with our psychic senses often accompany this process. We may pick up visual impressions about a soul's former earthly appearance; we may hear distinct voices with accents and gender; we may sense feelings being projected upon us; or we might simply channel written information, with no other impressions. Each experience will be different for each person.

1. **Stimulus:** Choose a soul that you would like to connect with, or learn more about. If you are not aware of any of your spiritual companions yet, ask Heaven to choose one to reveal to you.

2. **Response:** Switch into receiving mode, and then begin to record any and all impressions that come to mind, regardless of how unrelated, random, or obscure they seem. Many of these strange impressions will make sense after the writing session is completed. Continue to write every thought that passes through your mind until you feel that the flow has run its course.
3. **Synthesis:** Take a moment to clear your mind. Then go back and reread the information you just transcribed. Do the impressions add up to give you any understanding of the history or purpose of this soul in your life? Did you receive any validations or communication from familiar souls? How does the information sit with your intuition?

CASE STUDY #1: Learning Characteristics of Your Spiritual Family

1. **Stimulus:** "What are the characteristics and personality of my primary spiritual guardian?"
2. **Response:** In this case, impressions begin randomly and continue in the following way: " . . . flowers in a meadow . . . blue skies . . . Tinker Bell . . . then the image of a woman . . . long blonde hair, flowing in a soft wind as in slow motion . . . she looks off into the distance . . . she smiles at me sideways . . . such a feeling of comfort and love coming from her . . . she's beautiful . . . I see us holding hands . . . then children . . . playing, holding hands in a circle and dancing . . . she says: be near me . . ."
3. **Synthesis:** In this case, the writing process facilitated a stream of clairvoyant, clairaudient, and clairsentient impressions. The visual images that showed how the soul chooses to appear to us, the emotions experienced by the subject, and the actual communication with the soul made this a productive session. The subject in this

case later learned from one of her metaphysical teachers that her "joy" guide is a female who likes to be called "Daisy," which validated several impressions from the session. The subject also suspects that she shared a previous life with this soul, one in which the two were sisters.

CASE STUDY #2: Connecting with Loved Ones in Spirit

1. **Stimulus:** "My friend recently passed away unexpectedly. I would like to know that he is all right and still with us."
2. **Response:** Immediately the subject was filled with warm and fuzzy memories of her friend. She began recording her memories and then noticed a switch in tense, as the memories seemed to be interrupted by impressions of her friend sitting next to her on the bed: "He's sitting right next to me, laughing at me like he always does, like he's teasing me, or making jokes . . . he's telling me that it's all good . . . he's watching me write this and seems pleased to see the process working . . . he tells me not to worry about his family, that 'this was the agreement . . . it turned out to be a little tougher than we expected, but it's all right . . .'"
3. **Synthesis:** Again, the writing process served as a catalyst for a mediumistic experience. Memories often synthesize with psychic information when we are dealing with souls we knew personally in this life, so it is often difficult to be absolutely certain that our minds aren't deceiving us. Nonetheless, we are often given feelings or insights that can convince us of the genuine nature of the experience.

During these writing sessions you may find yourself amidst many different scenarios. You may find that you are receiving descriptions or imagery, names or events or verbal messages. You may be given information about previous lives of your guides, as well as their spiritual roles in your life. Ideally, information that you receive in this way should affirm or validate impressions you receive through meditation. You may have sensed your guide around you during meditation—you may have sensed his or her personality, or had a vision of his or her appearance. Inspirational writing can allow more specific detail to flow and help us to recognize the basic characteristics of the souls who live alongside us in our lives.

Investigating Past Lifetimes Through Writing

Past lives, if we believe in them, can be a source of both intrigue and self-understanding. Our past is the root of all that we are now. Our talents, our interests, our karma, our loved ones, and our enemies travel with us from life to life. Elements of our past lives are all around us in our present lives. However, if we are seeking a more profound understanding of our soul's history, we can employ our writing skills and our intuition to assist us.

1. **Stimulus:** Open your mind to any information that you might receive regarding a past life.
2. **Response:** Switch into receiving mode; then begin to record any thoughts or impressions, paying particular attention to any places, objects, clothing, or feelings you might receive. Continue to write down every thought that passes through your mind, until you feel that the flow has run its course.
3. **Synthesis:** Take a moment to clear your mind; then go back and reread what you wrote. How do you feel about the information? Is it consistent with any talents, themes, or subject matter relevant to your life today?

Do you feel connected with the information on an intuitive level?

CASE STUDY: Past-Life Awareness

1. **Stimulus:** "I would like to learn more about any past lives that are currently affecting my life situation and karmic issues."
2. **Response:** " . . . impressions of England, fog, wrought iron, an image of a man standing by a fire, working with hot metal; color, reds, rainy stone wall–lined streets . . . ."
3. **Synthesis:** The subject was intrigued by these impressions, as she had always felt drawn to England, and had lived there for a short time. She had also always been attracted to the look of wrought iron, stone, and other medieval styles of architecture or decorating. Months later, during a karmic astrology reading, she was told of a life she had previously lived as a male stained glass maker and craftsman in pre-Renaissance England.

Frequently Asked Questions

Question: "It is always a struggle to start writing. Nothing seems to come to me for a while, and I find myself struggling through the first few minutes with self-generated information. How can I get the information to get started faster?"

Explanation: At first, the information may seem clumsy or forced, possibly even unrelated. Do not let this hinder you. Push through this stage. This is how it feels when your psychic channels begin to open. We are not quite yet "in the zone," but we are on our way.

Solution: Continue to write, or ask more questions as necessary. Information will soon begin to flow freely.

Question: "What do I do when the flow stalls in the middle of a session?"

Explanation: Sometimes our rational thought processes interfere with the flow of the process. Or sometimes the flow breaks off on its own. In the first case, clear your mind and restart the process with no judgments or expectations. In the second case, you may have received all of the information on the subject that you are meant to have at this time.

Solution: Use your intuition to determine whether or not to proceed for more information. If you continue to receive nothing, then it is usually a message to move on to other subjects.

Question: "I try to connect with my mother, who has passed on, but I just get upset and I miss her so much that I end up just writing about my feelings of loss. What can I do?"

Explanation: This is a classic example of how our emotions interfere with the psychic process. This is also one of the primary reasons most people have trouble communicating with their loved ones who have passed. If we have an emotional reaction when we think of them, we have just created a state of static interference in our psychic senses. In this state our intuition is overpowered by our emotion, and it is often very difficult for the subtlety of intuition to shine through.

Solution: The only real solution to this situation is to come to better terms with our loved one's passing. This is not an easy fix. It may take time, even years, if it ever happens at all. Grieving is a profoundly difficult and individual process to work through. Grief counseling may assist us in understanding our loss and learning how to miss our loved ones without causing damage to ourselves.

Question: "How do I know that the intuitive process is working?"

Solution: When our intuition begins to kick in, we begin to feel a sense of inspiration within us. An energetic flow of information often becomes stronger and seems to carry us effortlessly along. Everything just flows through us and out of us. Whether we are writing, painting, speaking, making music, or involved in any other creative act, intuition, at its best, flows with the ease of inspiration.

Summary

Regardless of the reason we choose to write inspirationally, it can be a valuable process for self-discovery. We can gain insights into our selves and the situations surrounding our lives, as well as the higher planes of existence. Each person can find his or her own unique, natural way of utilizing this system of information retrieval, whether it is through journaling, typing, speaking into a tape recorder, or any other method. The more we experiment with our strengths and weaknesses, the sooner we will discover our fortes for spirit work.

Part Three

Illumination:
Advanced Intuitive Workshops

Think of yourself as an incandescent power, illuminated and perhaps forever talked to by God and his messengers.

—Brenda Ueland

I know this now. Every man gives his life for what he believes. Every woman gives her life for what she believes. Sometimes people believe in little or nothing and they give their lives to that little or nothing . . . But to sacrifice what you are and live without belief, that's more terrible than dying.

—Joan of Arc

CHAPTER 15

BECOMING THE MESSENGER: *Understanding Heavenly Messages*

As our intuitive talents blossom, an amazing thing happens. We find ourselves carrying within us a new belief in life, a kind of steady affirmation of life's meaningful nature that no longer eludes us. With everything we know; with everything the physical laws say we could never know; with every feeling we have that leads us through the darkness; with each experience that tells us that, yes, there is something more to this life, we feel Heaven living more and more within us.

There is no need for blind faith, because our experiences prove themselves. Every decision, every choice, and every adventure offers us a meaningful challenge. Everything means something. We are no longer standing on the sidelines, observing or trying to understand the spiritual world; we are taking part in it. We are no longer praying from a distance; we are living the process. We can live it, and we can share it with those we touch in our lives if they choose to accept it. We can be a light in the dark places. We can become the messenger for others who are waiting for word from beyond.

From Impressions to Messages

The first step in working with our intuition is recognizing our impressions. However, for the process to be complete, we must not only recognize the impressions but also learn to understand them and share them when necessary. This process takes time and patience. Heaven will speak to us each in unique ways; we must only take the initiative to understand the metaphors, symbols, validations, and feelings we are given. The language that Heaven speaks exists beyond our cluttered minds and dense thought vibrations, beyond our dull sensory experience. The meta-senses are our bridge across the dimensions. They are the link that allows us to tap into the subtle, harmonious vibrations of heavenly communication. Embracing this allows us to gather insights not only for ourselves, but for others as well.

Becoming the Messenger Workshop

It doesn't take much experience with intuition to realize that Heaven has a language of its own. It is a language that consists of more than words; it also comprises thought, symbols, colors, feelings, sound, and imagery. This multifaceted language is unique to each of us, based on our specific life experience. It is the language of our soul, and Heaven knows it even better than we do.

We can develop our understanding of this language by working with our intuition. The bottom line is always that Heaven will communicate with us in whatever way we will be most likely to understand, either literally or symbolically. The impressions and responses we receive from Heaven are like intuitive points of departure. We are given a piece of information, and then are faced with the task of extrapolating the appropriate meaning from that point. If we get it right, Heaven will continue to work with us using the same systems of symbols, sounds, or feelings, as appropriate. In this way, we develop a systematic method of communication with the spiritual realm.

Becoming familiar with this process will allow us to take the next step in our intuitive development, and will allow us to turn simple meaningful impressions into deeper meaningful messages. To do this, we can extend the Three-Step Intuitive Process of Intuition to a Five-Step Messaging Process.

The Five-Step Messaging Process

1. **Stimulus:** Ask for a message in the spirit of divine will.
2. **Response:** With quiet minds, we accept the first impression that comes to our mind, usually via one of our meta-senses.
3. **Determine the point of departure:** This first impression can be recognized as a point of departure, or a starting point of more in-depth message.
4. **Synthesis:** Use our intuition and our rational mind to extrapolate a general meaning from the point of departure, by interpreting it metaphorically or literally, usually based on our own life experience.
5. **Go with the flow:** Digress from this initial interpretation to apply it to the specifics of the personal situation at hand. Watch the point of departure widen into a meaningful, detailed life message, as intuition begins to flow. Intuitive information will soon begin to inspirationally flow through us as we speak. This process may be accompanied by additional psychic feelings that contribute to our understanding of the situation.

Many of us go through this process quite naturally in our everyday lives, without really knowing what we are doing. This intuitive process often inspires us when we are giving advice, solving problems, or helping friends through difficult situations. We may often find that, after a person asks our opinion on a situation, we suddenly find ourselves rambling on with all kinds of profound thoughts and advice. We may not even know the whole situation, but we get a feeling for it with our intuition. We have a sense of the proper course of action, and how to inspire the necessary choices, even though we may not have all of the facts. This is the intuitive process at work. We don't have to be "psychic" for Heaven to work through us.

Whether we are using our intuition instinctively or consciously, we become more adept with it each time we use it. Once we open the door to the light, more light shines in.

Tips for Using Our Intuition Consciously

The following ideas can assist us as we begin to intentionally work with our natural intuitive ability:

- This process can be used to gain insights for ourselves and our own personal situations, or for other people who wish to gain a higher perspective on certain elements in their own lives.
- When working intuitively with others, we will find that the process often works best with those whom we do not know intimately. The less we know about a person, the more certain we will be that we are bringing through genuine psychic information, not information based on what we already know about the person. For the same reason, it is often difficult to know we are bringing through genuine psychic information for ourselves.

Intuitive Messaging Through Clairvoyance

The following section will help us to understand visual impressions and how we can adapt their meaning to deeper life messages. Visual impressions will often be symbolic in nature and, like dreams, require interpretation. They may describe actual people, places, and things that are relative to our life or the lives of the people around us. Again, visual impressions are usually received in the mind's eye, just like a daydream. Once we receive an impression as a point of departure, all we must do is put the pieces of the puzzle together. Heaven will work with us, through repetition, to create our own language of impressions. Certain symbols can be used again and again, from message to message, when the same themes arise.

Tips for Intuitive Messaging Through Clairvoyance

- Always consider what the impression would mean to you, personally. Heaven will use our personal lives and experience as the basis of most impressions.
- Do not be surprised if many of the impressions you receive are based on popular culture or mass media—everything from road signs to movie scenes to fast food. Everything that we see from day to day is fair game for visual impressions. Visual impressions can also come in a series to literally spell out a message. For example, if we get an impression of a stop sign, and then a slab of meat, our message may be a very direct one regarding our health.
- You can interpret details of some visual impressions much as you interpret the meaning of a painting or other piece of artwork. There may be elements of color, composition, and implied action that reveal a deeper meaning.
- Don't forget your sense of humor. Heaven often throws jibes and jokes our way. Those impressions may confuse us if we take them too seriously.

Types of symbolic visual impressions and possible meanings

Impression	*Meaning*
Stop sign	Stop a certain course of action
Green light	Good prospects ahead
Yield sign	Proceed with caution
Hearts	Love and affection
Dove	Peace
Fireworks	Excitement and activity
Highway	Travel
Clock	Timing issues
Piggy bank / coins	Money
Books	Study/learning
Seedling	New growth
Sunrise	Beginnings
Sunset	Endings
Pregnancy	Birth/new life
Traffic	Busy time of life
Angel	Divine guidance
Storm	Troubles
Scales / yin-yang	Balance is needed
Flashing lights	Danger
Construction	Building up
Falling	Feeling lack of control
Crashing waves	Overwhelming emotional situation
Bird in cage	Oppression
Battle	Conflict
Balloons	Celebration or party
Gold rings	Marriage

Other Possible Types of Visual Impressions

- Scenes from movies, television, cartoons, or any type of mass media
- Visions of actual places or people or things
- Colors
- Letters or numbers seen in the mind's eye

CASE STUDY: How Clairvoyant Messages Are Received and Processed

1. **Stimulus:** A woman asks for a message, any message, that she can share with a friend.
2. **Response:** In her mind's eye, she receives, almost instantaneously, the impression of a kitchen. It just pops into her mind, so quickly that she nearly misses it altogether. The thought seems so random and out of the blue that she nearly lets it pass her by.
3. **Determine the point of departure:** She accepts the impression of the kitchen as her point of departure, and begins to focus on how that impression feels to her. She senses that it feels warm, is yellow, and that there seems to be a woman in it cooking food and setting a table. She "sees" all of this in her mind's eye, like a daydream or a memory.
4. **Synthesis:** Her rational mind begins to intervene, as she wonders what this kitchen could possibly mean to her friend. She wonders if she is seeing an actual kitchen, through remote viewing, or if this kitchen is a metaphor. She then realizes that she must release this debate and trust her intuition to guide her to the correct interpretation. She decides to proceed with the message by getting into the details of the kitchen in her mind. She feels its warmth. She feels comfort. She suddenly has a sense of the how good it feels to be taken care of, to be nurtured

and mothered. With each of these feelings she is gradually being led into the true meaning of the impression. She becomes aware of the kitchen as a metaphor for how we provide for our loved ones, how we nourish them and help them grow.

5. **Go with the flow:** As she discovers the meaning of her impression, she finds that, now that the correct door is open, information starts to flow freely. Almost as if she turned on a tap, the message comes through effortlessly. She tells her friend that she is sensing issues around her role as a caregiver. She also tells her friend that she senses much warmth and appreciation around her, that her efforts are truly appreciated by her loved ones, even though they may not acknowledge all that she does. She encourages her friend to continue providing in this role to the extent that she is comfortable, because she is planting seeds of love and affection in those she touches. The woman feels that, in this situation, her friend was in need of reassurance of the value of her role in nurturing the physical, spiritual, and intellectual health of her loved ones.

Intuitive Message Through Clairaudience

This section can help us to understand different kinds of auditory impressions and how we can adapt their meaning to deeper life messages. If we are naturally clairaudient, if we have an affinity for music, numbers, or language, we may find that many of our impressions come through words or sound. We may hear actual sounds or voices, or we may experience clairaudient impressions like thoughts—silently, in our mind.

Tips for Intuitive Messaging Through Clairaudience

The following tips will guide you as you receive auditory impressions:

- Like visual impressions, auditory impressions also can be translated literally or metaphorically. Words or phrases can be direct statements or can serve as analogies or metaphors, as in literature or poetry.
- Because they are most direct, verbal impressions are often a call to action. Don't be surprised if you receive the most urgent information via clairaudience. In emergency situations, it is worth Heaven's extra energy to force direct impressions that are less likely to be overlooked or misunderstood, instead of banking on our ability to sort out any convoluted symbols.
- Remember to suspend critical judgment during your intuitive moments. Accept the information Heaven provides you; then let it take you where it will. The more that you let go and trust where you are taken, the clearer and more accurate your intuition will become. Rationalization and doubt only create a static that leaves us blank and uninspired.

Possible Clairaudient Impressions as Points of Departure

- Songs and/or lyrics
- Famous quotations
- Actual voices
- Sounds
- Words, phrases, or letter sounds
- Advertising slogans or any information from mass media

CASE STUDY: How Clairaudient Messages Are Received and Processed

1. **Stimulus:** As he opens himself to Heaven, a man asks for an intuitive message for a woman he knows.
2. **Response:** The first thing that comes to his mind are words, almost like lyrics, that say love the one by your side, not the one you hide. The "memory" of the song—music and lyrics—just pops into his head, and continues to repeat as long as he focuses on it.
3. **Determine the point of departure:** He accepts the impression as his intuitive point of departure, and begins to focus on how that impression feels and what it means.
4. **Synthesis:** He begins to wonder if that song had special meaning to the woman, or if perhaps it is a direct message. Again, he remembers that he cannot answer that question with his reason, but must allow his intuition to take him to it. He lets go of his critical instinct, and concentrates on any feeling he gets from the impression. He soon feels that the song is a direct message, that there is someone the woman is missing.
5. **Go with the flow:** He decides to tell the woman about the impression of the specific song and lyrics, both to illustrate the point he is about to make and to allow for the possibility that the song also could have personal meaning for the woman. He explains that he senses that she is lonely for someone who had once been in her life. He feels that she is causing herself excess amounts of suffering by spending her time pining for what she does not have, instead of appreciating the life that is currently around her. He tells her that he feels that if she and the other person are not together now, it is for a reason concerning their souls' growth. She is inhibiting that

growth by clinging to fruitless longings and focusing on the abstract instead of the real. He feels that only by accepting the situation and recognizing the blessings in her life will she be able to attract the things she truly needs.

Other Means of Intuitive Messaging

Though clairvoyant and clairaudient impressions are commonly used psychic senses, we can receive intuitive information through any of our meta-senses, including physical sensations, emotions, smells, or tastes. We also can receive information through our intuition alone, via telepathy or precognition.

Other Kinds of Sensory Impressions as Points of Departure

There are many additional ways our bodies can receive impressions through sensory impressions:

- Actual physical sensations such as tingling or subtle pains in certain bodily areas
- Emotions such as joy, sorrow, fear, love, anxiety, peace, and so on
- Knowledge of specific future events
- Awareness of specific events or thoughts around a person

The examples of possible types of impressions are endless. Whatever intuitions we have, we should acknowledge and work with as much as possible. Impressions come through for a reason, not just for our amusement. Impressions can be as simple as a fleeting thought, or so intense that they may move us to tears. They can be so direct that their meaning is obvious, or so enigmatic that we may feel like we are solving a riddle. Each situation is unique; each message is unique. And we are only the messengers. We only deliver what we have been given. We need not understand it.

When the Message Isn't Getting Through

Heaven goes to great lengths to give us messages that we will understand. If only it were as easy for us to get them through our (often thick) heads. We may feel blocked. All the information we pick up may seem to be wrong. There may be times when we do not understand the messages or impressions we are given. Many times, these things will remain a mystery to us, and will pass away unresolved. But Heaven will not be so easily placated at other times. Some messages simply must get through. In the following cases, we can witness the persistence and fortitude of our friends in the spirit world. If at first they don't succeed, they will try and try again.

The Persistence of Heaven

The following are examples of just a few methods Heaven employs to get the message through when our own doubts or misunderstandings are standing in the way.

ONE HINT LEADS TO ANOTHER

Many times, if we fail to attach the proper meaning to an impression, Heaven will be kind enough to give us successive impressions that point us to the appropriate meaning. We get a hint, or a clue. If we still don't get it, we may get another.

CASE STUDY: When Heaven Persists

A woman is bringing through intuitive information for a colleague. During the session, she gets the visual impression of a cherry. Having no idea how to place such information, she makes the cardinal mistake: She disregards it, and attempts to move on. The next impression that comes through to her is the impression of a cherry pie. The impression is even rich with the smell and taste of a fresh-baked pie. Thinking (wrongly) that this impression was a false reaction to the previous false impression, she disregards this one too. (Meanwhile her friends in Heaven are shaking their heads.) Finally, she gets a clairvoyant impression of a butcher, but not just any butcher. The impression is a scene from the movie *Moonstruck* with Nicolas Cage. In the scene, he is in his butcher shop, talking to his co-star . . . none other than Cher. (Now, if she doesn't get this one . . .) It took three impressions to give her the confidence to go with the original word "cherry." Not knowing how else to approach such an obscure impression, she asks her colleague if "cherry" means anything to her. As it turns out, Cherry was the last name of a man the person knew, who had recently passed away.

This example should remind us all that no impression is too mundane or insignificant to be important information from Heaven. As well, our teachers and guides will employ even the most roundabout methods to get us to say a specific word or phrase. Be aware of this and any apparent connections between impressions. Successive impressions with a common thread usually indicate that Heaven is going to great lengths to reassure us and motivate us to pass on the message.

Heaven's Temper

When we don't get it, Heaven often delivers the message stronger, faster, and louder. Of course, there is no negative emotion involved, just increasing intensity. Our friends on the other side may not hesitate to drill us with repetition and persistence when we aren't heeding their call. It's just as in this world—if we can't hear someone, they speak to us louder and often repeat themselves emphatically. Our friends on the other side will do the same when we aren't "hearing" them.

CASE STUDY: When Heaven Insists

In this case, a man who is taking part in an intuitive development workshop is focusing on picking up any information for anyone in the room. During a quiet meditation, he receives the clairaudient impression of the name Henry. The subject asks the group if anyone can place the name Henry. No one can. Meanwhile, the impression continues in the subject's mind: Henry. And again: Henry. Then, he receives more creative impressions, like an Oh Henry! candy bar. The subject asks again, but still no one can place the name. At this point, Heaven offers some support impressions. The subject receives an impression of a man digging a hole and planting a tree in it. He shares this information with the group, but still no one can validate it. The subject decides to give it up and move on.

But Henry apparently doesn't want to move on. Whoever he is, he is not giving up, and is not about to let the man give up either. The impressions keep coming, the same name over and over again, each one feeling more emphatic—to the point that the man even hears the clairaudient impression "It's Henry, dammit!" with a whole lot of exclamation points. The image of a grumpy old man, wearing flannel, a cap, and bib overalls, begins to come through to the man. He tries very hard to figure out who this old fella is coming through for, but can think of no way to resolve the situation. They reach an impasse. The man can think of nothing else to do at the time other than to "turn off" his receptivity and proceed with his intuitive tune-out. He does so, while asking Heaven to assist him in any way possible with resolving poor Henry's frustration. Soon, Henry is gone and the man is left trying to place the information . . . somewhere.

He begins to wonder if, maybe, the message was one for his own life. He proceeds to ask friends and relatives if they ever knew a man named Henry who matched that description and who, apparently, had something to do with planting trees. Several days later, his mother informed him that the family had connections with an old farmer, who had since passed away, known as "Old Man Henry"—a farmer who sold them the trees that they planted at the family's first home.

There may be times when it is difficult to place or interpret subject matter, but Heaven will work with us as well as it can. It is most important that we do not give up. Very often the messages, as insignificant as they may seem, are very important to both the senders in the spirit world and the receivers in the physical world.

The Ambush

If we miss the message from our spiritual friends the first time around, we shouldn't be surprised if they show up again, when we least expect it. During certain seemingly mindless activities, such as driving, showering, gardening, or cleaning, our intuition may be inadvertently relaxed and open to psychic information. When this is the case, our guides or departed friends may take advantage of an opportunity to sneak in an impression or two, particularly if they have tried, unsuccessfully, to get a message through at an earlier time. When this happens, it is up to us to determine whether or not we are in an appropriate position to conduct spirit work. If we are not, we can ask politely that they return at another time, when we are choosing to work with our intuition. Otherwise, we can take advantage of the moment and proceed with our message work.

CASE STUDY: When Heaven Drops In

A man is receiving psychic information for a person he has just met, a woman who was intensely grieving the recent loss of her young husband. During this process, the man begins to receive impressions from the husband, who seems extremely excited to have this opportunity to communicate with his wife. The man passes on information and validations from the husband, who, more than anything, seems to be amazed that this process works. (Yes, those in spirit can be just as excited and amazed as we are at the prospect of genuine cross-dimensional communication.) Though some very important validations came through from the husband, the wife leaves the meeting feeling unsatisfied and somewhat betrayed by the fact that though the husband brought many messages, all she had really wanted to hear was that he loved her.

Several days later, while the man is cleaning his house, he feels the husband's presence with him, out of the blue. The man, though unaware of the wife's adverse reaction to the previous messages, allows the husband to add some closure. The subject receives a clairaudient message: "Tell her that I really, really love her." He delivers the message by phone the next day, without realizing how much the wife appreciates those words.

There are many reasons that may cause a soul to approach us outside of our normal spiritual routine. Some may have unfinished business. Some may be trying again when they had previously failed to get through to us. Some just do it because they can. Nevertheless, it is up to us to discipline ourselves and our spiritual companions as to the appropriate times and places that we choose to work with them. We should keep in mind that, though they might sneak up on us, we have the control and free will to accept them or to ask them to return another time.

Frequently Asked Questions

Question: "What do I do if I give people a message and they have no idea what I am talking about?"

Explanation: This is bound to happen from time to time. Often, people will be so excited about getting a message or reading that they forget a lot of information about their lives. This can be very frustrating to the intuitive process. There is a good chance that the person simply isn't connecting the information at that time.

Solution: If they do not understand the message (and you are fairly sure of what it is), ask them to take note of it and suggest to them that perhaps the meaning will connect with them at a later time. Also, ask Heaven for any other guidance that could clarify the situation for both of you. If more information comes, share it the best that you can. If not, then you have done as much as you can.

Question: "What do I do if I get impressions or messages for strangers?"

Explanation: This is, ultimately, a personal decision. However, we are on dangerous ground when we confront someone we do not know with profound spiritual information. The general consensus is to avoid this, unless you feel there is some really important reason you must share information with them.

Solution: If you absolutely can't hold back, *always* approach the person carefully and ask if he or she wants to receive the information before you start spouting off things like "your dead mother is standing next to you." This may be more than many people can handle. So, it is imperative to ask a person's permission before getting into any heavy conversations.

Question: "Is it okay to give intuitive messages when I don't have time to meditate or prepare myself?"

Explanation: That question can best be answered on a case-by-case basis by our own intuition. It is always preferable to be certain that we are in the proper state of mind for spirit work. Nonetheless, we also don't want to fall into any ritualistic traps.

We shouldn't feel that we can't make an intuitive decision unless we meditate for an hour first.

Solution: Let your intuition guide you as to the amount of preparation needed for each session, and do the best you can to keep yourself centered and protected in the process.

Summary

The language of our souls is simple at some times and requires our well-honed interpretive skills at others. Either way, it is always unique to us and speaks in the language of our own life and our own experiences. Our history creates us. Heaven uses the past to help us understand our future, and the future of those we meet. The more in touch we are with ourselves, the easier it will become to understand heavenly input.

The true fulfillment of reason as a faculty is found when it can embrace the truth simply and without labor in the light of single intuition.

—Thomas Merton (1915–1968), U.S. religious writer, poet; from "Reason and Reasoning," The Ascent to Truth, *Harcourt Brace (1951)*

CHAPTER 16

EVERYDAY EVIDENCE: *Confirming Intuitive Precision*

Once we have learned how to receive impressions, then understand them enough to pass them on or integrate them into our lives, we will become concerned with our accuracy. We all want to be sure that the process is genuinely working. We do not want to deceive anyone, including ourselves, or give anyone false information. We want to be certain that we understand the process completely before trying it out on friends or family members, who may already be questioning our sanity.

When we are working with our intuition, we are given a primary directive to trust our impressions, despite our fears or doubts about them. Some metaphysical schools will discourage the process of validation under the premise that, if we are too worried about getting our information right, we will corrupt the process altogether. Nevertheless, if we never get confirmation of our successful message work, we will not have full confidence in the process. We need this confidence to believe in the process. We need validation to know that this is *real.*

The following workshop outlines different kinds of sessions that assist us in validating the intuitive process, and how it works within us. Most of these exercises can be done as practice work, to help us develop on our own and prepare us for deeper work down the road.

Validation Workshop

Different Ways to Practice and Confirm Intuitive Accuracy

For us to nurture the growth of our intuition, we should use it as much as possible. The more we rely on our intuition, the more intuitive we become. We learn by doing. We can develop daily routines and practices that flex our intuitive muscles and allow us to be more aware and confident of our intuitive impressions. Just as artists keep daily sketchbooks, just as musicians practice the scales, we, as intuitives, can develop our art with daily practice.

Tips for Building Intuitive Reliability

- Remember, your intuition is working with you constantly. The trick is to recognize it and tune in to its patterns.
- The more you use your intuition, the easier it will seem to come to you.
- You may want to invent your own systems of practice based on your own sensibilities. Don't hesitate to be creative with new and interesting ways to validate your intuition.

Precognitive Clues

We can gain affirmations on a daily basis by working with simple intuitive impressions. This can be done at any time as we are going about our daily activities, particularly our somewhat mindless activities, like washing the dishes or going for a walk. Follow the three-step process, as you've done in other Workshops, in order to gain easily validated intuitions.

1. **Stimulus:** Clear your mind and ask Heaven to provide you with simple precognitive impressions that can be validated throughout the day.
2. **Response:** Notice any impressions that come to mind.
3. **Synthesis:** Make note of or record any impressions for reference throughout the day. Don't try to figure out their meaning ahead of time; just see how or if they play out throughout the day.

Types of Precognitive Clues

Daily Impressions

In the morning, when your day is fresh, quiet your mind. Then use your intuition to get an impression that will have significance for you throughout the ensuing day. This can be any kind of impression, like a visual symbol or object, or a phrase, or a song—any simple impression. Most likely, whatever you receive will make little or no sense to you until later in the day when the meaning is revealed. For example, you may get the symbol of a penguin. Initially, this may seem like an arbitrary concoction of your imagination. Later in the day, however, it will take on new meaning when you receive a greeting card from a special person, with a penguin on the front. Or perhaps you end up getting tickets to a hockey game in Pittsburgh, or you see a meaningful movie scene that involves penguins. Daily symbols, when used in this way, can lead to greater levels of precognition.

COLOR IMPRESSIONS

When you are planning to meet a person, work with your intuition to discover what color of clothing they will be wearing when you see them. Ask this question to yourself, then note the very first thought that comes to your mind. If you have a strong clairvoyant psychic sense, then this task may come relatively easily. You can learn to understand how impressions feel, and can also build confidence with your successes. We can get color impressions for anything we like—clothing, vehicles, buildings, or any other material object we might encounter. If you have little luck, or find this to be frustrating, try a different exercise in this list.

DIRECTIONS

Next time that you are traveling to a new destination and are unsure of the route, try using your intuition. Trust the first direction, clue, or prompt that comes to mind. It may be a simple "turn left" or it may be a symbol or name of something else nearby. It may even be a simple *feeling* that you should go in a certain direction. Our intuition can be our savior when we are lost, either physically or spiritually.

OTHER TYPES OF PRECOGNITIVE CLUES WE CAN ASK FOR

- Events or themes of the day
- Key words or topics in conversation during the day
- Objects or numbers of importance
- People you will interact with
- Moods people will be in that day
- Kinds of cars people will be driving
- What people will look like before you meet them
- Times that certain events might occur

Name Billets

A billet is a small piece of paper, upon which we write down specific information that we wish to work with intuitively. When we create a group of billets, then shuffle them together, we create an anonymous pool of subject matter upon which to exercise our intuition. We pull a billet, without looking at what is written on it, then see what intuitive impression follows as we focus upon it. This process allows us to be objective when receiving intuitive information, since we are "blind" to its contents. We rely on Heaven to know what is on the card and to give us the necessary input. This process is a great way to practice and affirm our intuitive ability on our own.

1. Select a group of ten to twenty people with whom you feel connected in your life. These could be any friends, family members, loved ones, coworkers, or any other significant people in your current life or from your past.
2. Write down each of their names on a separate index card, or piece of paper. Then turn the cards over, or fold the paper, so that the names cannot be seen.
3. Shuffle them around until you are no longer consciously aware of where any of the names are.
4. Close your eyes and then pick a card that you are drawn to.
5. Hold the card in your hand as you open your intuition to any feelings or thoughts that will come to mind. You may want to hold the card over the third-eye or heart chakra to enhance psychic receptivity (see Chapter 11).
6. Record any impressions you receive while holding the paper in your hand. Do not concentrate on figuring out whose name is on the card, but instead allow your impressions to flow without judgment.

7. When you feel that you have received enough information, open your eyes and read the name on the card.
8. Try to understand how the impressions that you were receiving are connected to that individual. Did you feel connected with that person before you read the card? Did you receive any information specific to that person, such as impressions to clue you in to his or her identity? This process enables you to understand how your own intuition communicates with you. By doing this often, you will get a better feel for your intuitive style, and will receive many validations of the intuitive process.

CASE STUDY #1: Billets and Visual Metaphor Clues

While holding a name billet, a man gets an impression of wires and a keyboard. Though he's initially stumped as to the meaning, he understands it when he turns the card over to find the name of a friend who works for a technology company.

CASE STUDY #2: Billets and Sound Clues

In a similar situation, a woman notices Pachelbel's Canon suddenly going through her mind. She turns the card over to learn that she has the name of her sister, who often played the piece on the piano.

CASE STUDY #3: Billets and Names

As a young woman is practicing this exercise, the letters *JN* pop into her mind. She turns the card over to find the name "Jen" written on the other side. Often, letters will lead us to pronunciation, more so than spelling.

In all of these cases, we can see how Heaven was leading us to the correct subject matter. We can't expect it to point us to the obvious, but instead to lead us in the right direction. It is up to us to make the leap that finally connects us to the actual meaning. This exercise is a great way to practice attaching our impressions to their meanings.

Frequent Problems

Problem: "I seem to get strong impressions, but I can't make the right sense of them."

Explanation: Knowing your impression is half the battle. Once you are sure of your impressions, you can learn to understand them better through practice. You will begin to understand the subtle and specific ways that your own intuition works. Once you become more aware of that process, you will become more adept at attaching the right meaning to your impressions.

Solution: Practice, practice, practice!

Problem: "The impressions I get aren't usually the most obvious impressions I would associate with the person on the billet."

Explanation: For some reason, Heaven very rarely gives us the information that we would expect to get. Perhaps this is to keep us on our toes; perhaps it is to reinforce to us that we aren't cheating or creating the information ourselves. Spiritual experiences are often not at all what we might expect. In many ways, this is a validation of its own: The experience is genuine because, we, ourselves, could not have conceived of it.

Solution: Release your expectations and accept whatever information Heaven offers.

Summary

Validations, even of the most seemingly insignificant nature, are important steppingstones as we build confidence in our inner guidance. Any routines or processes we establish to validate our intuition on a regular basis will assist in our psychic growth, as well as our understanding of how we receive impressions. Practice makes perfect.

To the poet, to the philosopher, to the saint, all things are friendly and sacred, all events profitable, all days holy, all men divine.

—Ralph Waldo Emerson

CHAPTER 17

SACRED OBJECTS AND PSYCHOMETRY

Sacred Objects

All things that exist in the material world carry with them a history of the kinds of energy that they have come in contact with. In addition, the molecular composition of certain objects is such that they actually amplify surrounding energy, or store it. These objects have taken on a special status throughout history because of their ability to assist with spiritual processes or understanding. Crystals, pendulums, gemstones, or personal objects, through psychometry, can be valuable tools to assist the intuitive process.

Crystals

Quartz crystals are one of the most popular metaphysical tools, primarily because of the powerful ways that they work with energy. Crystals amplify, transform, transmit, focus, and store energy. We can find crystals in such practical technologies as televisions, watches, lasers, computers, and satellites. Crystals can increase electrical signals, transform energy to waves, or concentrate energy into a powerful focus.

This powerful ability extends itself not only to science and technology, but also to our human physiologies. Our bodies are electric. The electric energy that vibrates through us responds to crystals, just as does the electric energy of our technological instruments. In this way, we can utilize crystals in our own life to amplify, transform, transmit, focus, and store our own personal energies.

Emotions and thoughts fuel these energies and determine how our spiritual energy vibrates and resonates. As we begin to work with crystals we may gain an understanding of how they affect our thoughts and emotions by affecting our energy field. Whatever state we are in when we work with crystals will generally be amplified, whether that state is balanced or imbalanced. Therefore, we should be very careful to be centered and clear when we do our crystal work. If we are at peace with ourselves, we may find that crystals raise our vibration and empower us. If we feel anxiety or fear, we may only notice this negative energy increasing if we do not take the proper steps to balance our energy before working with the crystals.

In regard to intuition, crystals have been utilized to amplify and transmit psychic energy. They can assist in our meditation by helping us to harmonize our mental energies. They can assist in our intuitive processes as a transmitter of psychic information. With crystals, we may see more clearly and feel more strongly. The age-old archetype of the fortuneteller with a crystal ball has its roots in the clairvoyant enhancement that crystal has been known to offer us. Whether we are using crystal as a gazing ball or in smaller pieces as psychic amplifiers, it can produce considerable results.

Gemstones

Throughout history precious stones have been prized both for their beauty and for the mystical powers they are said to impart upon their wearers. When worn or kept in our personal space, gemstones can transmit subtle energy vibrations into our aura. Each stone may resonate in specific ways and touch in with our chakras.

Each of us may be intuitively drawn to the specific types and colors of stones that can serve to balance, harmonize, and heal our etheric energies. This is particularly true of jewelry. We may be inclined to wear specific jewelry at certain times in our lives, and then shy away from the same jewelry at other times for no apparent reason other than that we don't *feel* like wearing it. As we carry these stones with us throughout our days, they work to balance us in subtle ways. Stones can also be used during meditation to assist us in achieving the states of mind or being that we strive for, such as peace, harmony, strength, creativity, or intuitive openness.

The inherent qualities of gemstones are utilized through modern technology with the use of crystals in watches, lasers, and computers, but their more subtle effects, such as their ability to promote physical healing in the body or their power to help balance human emotions, still elude traditional science. Nonetheless, we understand that the energies within gemstones interact with our own scientifically imperceptible energies to create the effects we observe.

Pendulums

A pendulum consists of an object that is suspended from a fixed point. The object swings back in forth in response to gravity or other unseen forces. The Italian physicist and astronomer

Galileo established that once a pendulum is in full swing, its oscillation will remain the same, perpetually—a concept that became a cornerstone in the process of timekeeping.

Pendulums can be an interesting source of spiritual information and validation. The idea is that a suspended weight held in our fingertips will respond to information from our higher selves with unsolicited motion. In this way, most of the information derived from pendulum use is asked or received in a diametric manner—as a yes or a no, as a positive or a negative expression of energy. The pendulum may swing one way for a positive indication, another for a negative indication, or may not swing at all. To some extent, each individual develops his or her own pendulum language.

The pendulum itself does not act as an independent agent, but is guided by our own soul energies, along with any other energy it may be responding to. We can use the pendulum to seek inner guidance, or even to detect imbalances in our chakras or our aura. When a pendulum hangs from a hook on its own, it remains still. When we hold it quietly in our fingertips, it will seem to take on a life or motion of its own as it begins to respond to surrounding energies. The responses we receive from pendulum work are often an excellent validation for our intuition.

Care of Sacred Objects

The most important factor in maintaining our sacred objects is that we treat them with respect. Whatever systems or rituals we develop to use and store them is perfectly acceptable, providing that they are kept in a safe and uncontaminated environment. The following suggestions may provide some inspiration for safekeeping of our sacred objects.

Storing Sacred Objects

We should find a unique and special place to store our sacred objects. We can acquire beautiful, ornate wooden boxes or beaded pouches designed specifically to hold such objects. Or we can use items already on hand that have special meaning to us, such as scarves or old purses. Regardless, we should choose something special as our oracle's home, then keep it there always.

Handling Sacred Objects

Some people choose to let no one other than themselves handle their sacred tools. Others are comfortable sharing them with just about anyone. Again, the choice is ours. We should do whatever complies with our intuition.

Cleansing Sacred Objects

We can restore the energy in our objects, and should do so periodically to maintain energy vibrancy and purity.

While we may or may not choose to utilize sacred objects during our intuitive work, they are always available to us as a source of additional spiritual guidance. They should be taken seriously at all times, because they are not tools for our amusement or entertainment. They are, instead, profoundly spiritual vehicles for inner guidance. When taken as such, they can be of great value to our spiritual fulfillment.

Sacred Objects Workshop

The first step in preparation for any sort of spiritual work is to prepare ourselves. The next step is to choose and prepare any tools we will be working with. We may choose to work with no tools at all, but if we do decide to work with a particular tool, we should be sure that we are using it wisely and carefully.

Tips for Working with Sacred Objects

The following tips will help you as you continue your work with sacred objects:

- Each person will have different preferences regarding the sacred tools they work with. You may want to experiment with different tools to find out which one suits you best.
- Remember that objects such as crystals will enhance whatever energy you are dominantly working with, so it is important to use them wisely, and only when you are in a centered and balanced emotional state.
- To learn more about the specifics of sacred objects and energy work, you many want to consult one of the books on the market that contain detailed listings and descriptions of the specific properties and powers of crystals, gemstones, or other sacred objects.

Crystals

Crystals benefit us simply by being in our proximity. Their presence, particularly through touch, is enough to assist our energy flow. Crystals can be worn as jewelry or carried in a pouch or pocket throughout our daily activities.

We may also work with crystals during our meditation in order to enhance our focus, as well as to stimulate our intuitive receptivity and projections. You may simply hold the crystal in your hands as you allow your energy to flow through your palms; you may also hold it to other powerful energy centers, particularly the chakras or the third-eye area. Your intuition will guide you to the best way to utilize crystals during your spiritual work. Your task is to remain open and receptive to the process.

If you choose to work with crystals in order to assist in your intuitive work, you must first be sure you have the crystal that's best for you.

Choosing Your Crystal

Your intuition is your most reliable guide for choosing the right crystal.

1. Ideally, you should find a local store or event where crystals are sold, so you can select your crystal in person. Doing this allows you to hold the crystal, and get a feel for it, before you purchase it.
2. Place the crystal in the palm of your hand. Notice how you feel. Do you *feel* a connection with its energy? Does it *feel* like the right crystal for you? The connection may be particularly good if you notice any warmth or tingling sensations surrounding it. When you find a good crystal, you will simply know it.
3. Sometimes our crystals come to us. If you receive a crystal as a gift, or have an opportunity to buy a certain crystal, this, too, may simply be a part of divine order. As long as the crystal fits your vibration, you should be comfortable with it.

Cleaning Your Crystal

The crystals that we purchase through retail have been handled by numerous people, from shoppers to merchants to the person who actually mined them. A crystal absorbs energy like a sponge, so it is essential to purify any crystal before using it. Cleaning a crystal primarily involves clearing it of any residual thought energy that it may have accumulated from previous handlers or circumstances.

1. **Rinse with water and sea salt:** Gently wash the crystal with a mixture of water and sea salt. The water will cleanse it of any residue, and the sea salt will neutralize any energy contained within. Lightly polish dry.
2. **For stronger cleansing:** The crystal may be stored in a natural container of dry sea salt for several days. This is not necessary unless the crystal feels as though it needs intense purification.
3. **Additional cleansing methods:** Your crystal can be purified by holding the object directly in the smoke produced by burning sage, incense, or even a candle. You can also purify a crystal by exposing it to nature. Place it in direct sunlight, moonlight, out in the rain, or in the running water of a stream. You can even bury it in the earth for several days. Any of these methods will help to restore the crystal to its natural, neutral state.

Connecting with Your Crystal

Once your crystal is clean, you can begin to make your own connection with it. The more that it is kept within your energy field, the more your energy will saturate it. With time, the crystal will be attuned to your own personal energy vibration, and thus serve you as a perfectly customized sacred tool.

1. **Wear your crystal:** If possible, wear your crystal or carry it in your pocket every day.

2. **Sleep with your crystal:** At least during the first few weeks of ownership, try to keep the crystal next to your bed or under your pillow during the night.
3. **Tune in to your crystal:** Take some quiet time to connect with the energy inherent in your crystal, and to infuse your own energy into it. Hold it in your palms and become familiar with it. Notice how it looks and feels, as well as how you may feel when it is in your hands.

Using Your Crystal

You can use your crystal any time you like. Since the nature of the crystal is to amplify, you may find that, while you are amplifying your intuitive perceptions, you may inadvertently amplify any dominant thoughts or emotions in the process. If you are not mentally and emotionally balanced when you are working with your crystal, you may experience subtle emotional or psychological discomfort and may find yourself heightening whatever state you are in. If you are fearful or anxious, you may become more afraid or worried; if you are calm and at peace, your tranquility may become more pervasive. As always, the clearest channel is the best channel.

Gemstones

Gems, like crystals, can be powerful tools for balancing the emotional, mental, and spiritual aspects of our lives. In this way, our jewelry, in particular, may affect us more than we know. By choosing the right stones for our jewelry, we can effectively align ourselves with the best types of conductors for our personal energy.

Much time and energy has been dedicated to categorizing gems and the meaning held within the different types of stones. There are many systems of gemology in practice today. The following is but a brief description of the general capacities in which specific gems can serve us.

Agate: Enhances vitality; imparts strength and courage

Amber: Stimulates the intellect; assists in releasing the old and embracing the new

Amethyst: Calms the mind; enhances willpower; amplifies thought

Aquamarine: Enhances self-expression; reduces fear; balances throat chakra

Bloodstone: Stone of courage; promotes grounding

Citrine: Tempers energy of the power chakra; increases clarity with higher self

Diamond: Enhances endurance and fidelity; promotes unity and love

Emerald: Enhances intuition and balances heart chakra; creates harmony

Fluorite: Relieves stress and emotional blockages/negativity

Garnet: Increases creative energy of the second chakra; balances sexual energy

Hematite: Improves memory and dissolves negative energy

Jade: Stimulates rejuvenation; amplifies divine, unconditional love

Labradorite: Reduces stress; provides clarity of mind and focus

Lapis Lazuli: Promotes spiritual growth and intuition

Malachite: Assists in healing; promotes acceptance, loyalty, and responsibility

Moonstone: Promotes peace and harmony; balances emotions

Onyx: Absorbs and neutralizes negative energy; enhances self-control

Opal: Enhances intuition and mystical ability; promotes faith and harmony

Pearl: Enhances integrity and truth; alleviates emotional imbalance

Quartz: Assists with clarity of thought

Rose Quartz: Heightens unconditional love and self-esteem

Ruby: Enhances love and passion; improves health

Sapphire: Increases sensitivity to beauty and intuition; alleviates depression

Tiger's Eye: Promotes clarity of perception and balance

Topaz: Provides strength in overcoming fears and trust in divine will

Turquoise: Native American stone; heightens spiritual attunement; calms the mind

The type of gemstones that we choose to wear or carry may say more about our emotional and psychological states than we are consciously aware. Rely on your intuition to steer you toward the gemstones that are right for you.

Pendulums

With time and patience, most anyone can learn the art of the pendulum. When the pendulum is employed as a sacred tool, it will generally respond to us in one of three ways: as an expression of positive energy flow (yes), as an expression of negative or blocked energy flow (no), or as a neutral or static energy flow. The more intimate and experienced we are with our pendulum, the more detail we will be able to extrapolate from its movements. The emphasis and number of swings or turns can provide us with additional insights.

The pendulum, like all of the other sacred tools, has a personal language for each of us. As long as we know the meaning behind our pendulum's movements, it does not matter if that meaning conforms with other textbook indications. We should develop a system and abide by it, allowing our intuition to guide us along the way.

Choosing Your Pendulum

Choosing a pendulum is a lot like choosing a crystal—your intuition will guide you to the right one. It doesn't matter whether your pendulum is made from a paper clip attached to dental floss or from the finest cord and crystal. The only thing that matters is that you are spiritually connected with your pendulum. After you acquire a pendulum, spend some time connecting with it, as described for crystals and gemstones, until you feel that your energy has been comfortably integrated into it. Don't allow others to use your pendulum, because their energy may disrupt the system of energy flow you have already established with the device.

Learning the Language of Your Pendulum

By following these steps, you can learn more about how your pendulum speaks to you:

1. To begin, hold the pendulum by its cord with your thumb and first finger, about 3 inches from the weight at the end.
2. Quietly center yourself, or enter into a meditative state. Be sure that the pendulum, like your thoughts and emotions, is still.
3. Begin to concentrate on a positive energy flow. Envision anything connected with unimpeded manifestation and

with the "yes" response. This could include symbols and imagery like a green light or even the word "yes"—anything that will cause your energy to manifest through the pendulum as a positive. Notice any motion the pendulum begins to take on, specifically the direction of its swing. Most often, the positive energy flow will create a clockwise swing.

4. Next, quiet your pendulum. Then envision a blocked energy flow, associated with "no." You could visualize a red light, or any other symbol that would indicate a disruption in the positive flow. The motion of the pendulum should be different from the motion in Step 3. It could be a counterclockwise swing, it could be a back-and-forth or side-to-side motion, or it could be still. Again, it doesn't matter which combination manifests for you, as long as it manifests the same way consistently.
5. Quiet your pendulum once again. Then envision a neutral state, a quiet state of inactivity. This state represents a neutral response to the energy of a situation. Oftentimes, the pendulum will be still. Whatever the response, it should, again, be different from the previous two responses.

If you only experience irregular movement, quiet your mind and begin again. It may take some time and patience to get into the flow. Be sure to concentrate and focus your thought energy specifically on your intention. Once you have established the way your energy manifests through the pendulum, you can begin to use it to accompany the intuitive process.

It is wise to retest your pendulum language from time to time, because it, like our free will, is always subject to change.

Working with Your Pendulum

Pendulums have a vast array of uses, both scientific and spiritual. They have been the basis of clocks and metronomes for hundreds of years. They are used to measure the acceleration of gravity, as well as to prospect for oil, water, or other underground commodities. They are even used to assist in holistic healing and diagnosis.

For our metaphysical purposes, the pendulum can be viewed as an extension of our intuition. The energy from our higher self manifests through the physical motion of the pendulum, thus giving our intangible thoughts a sort of tangible reality. When we meditate or are working with our intuition, we can employ the pendulum as a validation of our impressions. By noting the type of movement the pendulum takes on in response to our thought energy, we can gain insight into the flow of energy that surrounds the people, places, and situations in our lives. When used wisely, the pendulum can be a valuable tool to help us develop our inner awareness and perceptive abilities.

Summary

No matter how we choose to use our psychic tools, it is always wise for us to keep in mind that no system of divination, no oracle, is designed to make our choices for us. We can work with our tools in a healthy and balanced fashion when we understand them as both a source of intuitive inspiration and spiritual guidance. They never are a means of absolute decision-making. Psychic tools can draw our attention to the fears and motivations that shape our life choices. Once we are more aware of ourselves, we will be more inclined to make better choices on our future path.

Psychometry

Psychometry is based on the notion that physical objects, when in direct contact with our personal energy fields, can enhance psychic perceptivity. All objects carry frequencies, and all frequencies can be understood through psychic energy. These frequencies may affect us as imprints from human energy that has been transferred to the objects, or the objects themselves may be conductors of energy that enhances overall psychic receptivity.

Psychometry has been called the art of seeing through touch. As we interface our own energy with that of a psychically charged object (simply through touch), we may begin to receive information about the history of that object or the people intimately associated with it. The life force that pervades the human body manifests through a field of electromagnetic energy. When objects come into frequent contact with that energy, they absorb elements of its frequency into their own physical makeup. This creates an energy imprint. The stronger the emotions during the time of exposure, the stronger the imprint upon the object will be. Therefore, it is not unusual to pick up pivotal life situations, such as moments of emotional trauma or ecstasy, when we examine personal objects.

The most popular type of psychometric objects is jewelry. Our rings, bracelets, and necklaces have usually spent long periods of time in the personal body space of their owners. In addition, metal is a natural conductor that easily absorbs and transfers psychic imprints. If jewelry is not available, we can gather intuitive information from a person's clothes, furniture, pictures, artwork, or important household items. Handwriting samples also can serve as a valuable source of psychometric energy.

It is speculated that psychometry has been in practice since ancient times, but the terminology and theory were introduced in the mid-1800s by J. Rhodes Buchanan, a scientist and professor of physiology. His theory of psychometry is based on the notion that all of our thoughts and actions leave permanent impressions on the ether, as well as the physical objects in their proximity. In this way, objects can store and transmit energies that are seemingly imperceptible to our five physical senses.

This process is one of the most effective ways to assist the intuitive flow. When we hold a personal object in our hand we expose ourselves to vibrations from its owner, which can directly affect our meta-senses. We may have stronger clairvoyant visions or may receive more audible clairaudient impressions. In general, our psychic feelings may be amplified. We may even sense that our mood changes as we hold the object. The energy that is transmitted to us during this psychic process can deepen our intuitive understanding of most heavenly communication.

Psychometry Workshop

Though anyone can learn the art of psychometry, it will come easier to some than others. Those of us who are strongly clairsentient will have a natural affinity for this process; the rest of us just may need to be a little more patient. We experience psychometric feelings every day, whether we are conscious of it or not. Every object or place that we come into contact with carries with it afterimages, or energy imprints, left over from previous times.

If we find ourselves with unexplained feelings of sorrow or anxiety when we tour places of tragedy, we are using our psychometric function. Many naturally intuitive people will have a disaffinity for antiques, which often carry strong vibrations from their previous owners. We use psychometry when we choose which clothing to wear. Clothes we bought years earlier will still carry with them the energy from the time when we wore them most, which may affect how we feel when we put them on. This explains why certain clothes may just not "feel" right, even though they look good, or are of good quality. The same can apply to objects and personal items that we carry with us throughout our lives. Some of our most special items will feel special to us because of the significance they had at a certain moment in our lives.

The following sessions are designed as opportunities to explore psychometry and how it works through the five metasenses. When we are touching in with the energy of an object, we can experience impressions from any of our different psychic faculties. Don't be surprised to experience symbols or feelings or verbal impressions. We will do best if we acknowledge any information that comes through us.

Object Trade

This is the most popular way to use psychometry. The idea is that, by holding an object that belongs or once belonged to another person, we will be able to psychically connect with the energy imprint that remains on that object.

Choose an object that has had only one owner. Otherwise, you may get mixed impressions. You may choose objects from people who have transitioned to the spiritual world, such as old clothes, jewelry, or personal items, or you may choose objects from anyone you know in your life now. Impressions from the former are likely to give you information about the deceased person's life on earth, and may also assist in the process of mediumship. Impressions from the latter are most likely to help you tune in to experiences in the life of the person during the most recent times that they were in contact with that object. If you want to pick on up on energy around a current situation, be sure to choose an object that is currently a part of a person's life.

Preparation

Quiet your mind and relax your senses. Pick up the object, and get to know it. You may want to touch it, feel it, in all of its nooks and crannies. You may even want to hold it close to your body, to your third-eye or heart chakra, depending on where you are most sensitive.

1. **Stimulus:** When you feel comfortable with the object, hold it in your nondominant hand, which is your receiving hand, or rest your nondominant hand on the object if it is too large to hold in the palm.
2. **Response:** Close your eyes, taking deep cleansing breaths as you open to your intuition. Continue to focus on the object while remaining in this state of openness. Impressions will come when the moment is right. Do not try to force it, and don't miss it when and if it does arrive.
3. **Synthesis:** Communicate or transcribe any information that you receive as soon as possible, while it is fresh in your mind. You may receive information about feelings that surrounded the object, as well as events, other people, or situations. Be open to anything. Then follow through to find as many validations for your impressions as possible.

Many people find that using psychometry in this way simply assists their natural intuitive function. We may receive impressions during this process in much the same way that we would whenever we use our psychic senses. The presence of the physical object may simply allow that energy to flow more intensely.

Photo-Sensitivity

Photographs can often be interesting and enlightening psychometry subjects. It is possible to sense distinct energy from a photograph, based on the circumstances surrounding its creation.

Preparation

To begin, gather a pool of photographs, old or new, but preferably filled with various people and places that are familiar to you. Turn the photographs face-down and mix them together or shuffle them, so that your conscious mind has no awareness of where each photo is located.

1. **Stimulus:** Choose a photo; then get comfortable with it. Feel it. Then hold it in your nondominant hand.
2. **Response:** Allow your impressions to flow, picking up on any energy that might be emanating from a particular photograph. Record any images, feelings, words, or impressions that come to mind. Do not try to guess which picture you are holding, even if you have an idea of which one it is based on the impressions you receive. If you try to guess the picture, and guess wrong, your critical mind will filter or distort any genuine energy that is coming through. Always remain open.
3. **Synthesis:** When you have received as much information as you will get, look at the photograph. Try to understand why you got the impressions that you did, and how they relate to the picture or the people in the picture.

Did you pick up on any dominant shapes or colors in the picture? Did you pick up any feelings or emotions associated with the situation involved? Did you sense any letters or words that may be in the picture? Did you get any information about the people or places in the photograph? Answering questions like these will tell you much about the way that you, specifically, receive psychometric information, and can provide validation of your intuitive ability and progress.

Color Cards

This exercise allows us to use psychometry to sense vibrations from color. When ink is laid down upon a surface, it creates a vibration from the frequency and intensity of the light that is absorbed in or reflected from the ink. We can sense this subtle energy with our psychic senses.

Preparation

Gather a set of index cards. Put a different color on each card, using ink, paint, crayon, or colored pencil. Then turn the cards face-down, and mix them up.

1. **Stimulus:** Choose a card. Hold it in your hand, but do not look at the color on the opposite side. Touch it. Feel the energy that emanates from it.

2. **Response:** Notice what impressions come to mind. Again, do not focus on figuring out the color, but only on receiving the impressions.

3. **Synthesis:** Try to determine the color on the card, based on your previous impressions. You may see the color in your mind's eye, or you may not. Generally, you will receive impressions that will lead you to the color—impressions that will train you to process psychic information abstractly, instead of merely translating what you are given. For example, if the color is "blue,"

you may receive the clairsentient impression of "coolness" or "coldness," or even "melancholy" or "sadness." Or you could receive clairvoyant impressions like "ice" or "sky" or even something whimsical like "Blue's Clues." You might even think of or taste blueberries. The possibilities are endless. But the key is to understand that the impressions you receive will lead you to your validation, even if they don't give you the easy answer. Heaven will always point us in the right direction. It is up to us to use our minds and wills to follow through to our destination.

The Signature of Handwriting

Our handwriting is probably the most readily available opportunity for psychometry, and also the most often overlooked. Our writing is a direct manifestation of our personal energy and reveals many things about how we channel that energy through our lives. Whether or not we are familiar with handwriting analysis, we can pick up distinct vibrations from a person's signature, or any other writing sample.

If you are using your intuition to touch in with psychic information about a specific person, it can be beneficial to ask for a sample of his or her handwriting on a piece of paper. When you hold that paper in your hands, you are also holding an imprint of the person's energy—one that may assist or direct the intuitive process in a specific way.

The following is an exercise you can employ to practice picking up energy from handwriting.

Preparation

Collect handwriting samples from a group of friends or acquaintances. The samples must be originals, no photocopies or computer printouts. You may cut up old cards or letters or grocery lists, or you may ask for original samples from different people. The more similar the paper stock is on each sample, the better. The idea is for the signatures to remain free of any associations, as were the colors and photos in the previous exercises. Any inconsistencies in the paper may cause your rational mind to interfere with your intuitive perceptions. Mix up the writing samples so that you may choose one without knowing whose writing is on the paper.

1. **Stimulus:** Select one card and hold it in your nondominant hand.
2. **Response:** Let your intuition flow. Note any impressions or feelings that come upon you. Do not try to guess whose handwriting you are sensing; concentrate only on receiving your intuitive information.
3. **Synthesis:** Record your impressions; then look at the paper to identify the writer. Identify the ways in which the impressions you received were related to the person whose handwriting is on the paper. Did you receive symbols or images that would be associated with that person's vocation or appearance or personality? Did you receive any impressions of names or letters in that person's name? Did you have any feelings that would connect you to that person specifically? Were you able to ascertain which person it was, before you revealed it to your conscious mind?

The more advanced we become in our sensitivity, the more likely we will be to find the distinct meaning of our impressions. In the meantime, we should not be frustrated if we fail to know the right name, or color, when it is hidden from us. The important thing is to understand the information that is coming through, bit by bit. The better we are at understanding that, the better we will become at intuiting the end result.

Frequently Asked Questions

Question: "What kinds of objects are suitable for psychometry?"

Explanation: You can use any object that has spent a significant amount of time in the energy field you are touching in with, although metal seems to be a particularly good conductor of the psychic energy. Watches and jewelry are excellent for this purpose, but you can really use anything, from handwriting samples to clothing and even furniture.

Solution: Use whatever you have!

Question: "Is there a particular way I should hold the objects or cards when I work with psychometry?"

Explanation: Most people recommend holding the object or card in your nondominant hand, because this is your receiving hand, although the process should work regardless of which hand you use. Some people like to hold the object near one of their dominant psychic receiving centers, as well. For example, if you are strongly clairvoyant, you may feel inclined to hold the card or object up to your forehead, in the region of your third eye. If you are a psychic "feeler," you may want to hold it close to your solar plexus. You may even find yourself instinctively doing these things, without really being aware of it.

Solution: Let your intuition guide you as you proceed with the objects or cards. If you feel an instinct to move the object close to a particular part of your body, go with it. Do whatever feels natural to you.

Question: "I don't really feel comfortable using crystals or other objects. Is that wrong?"

Explanation: There is no *need* to use any physical object or system to assist you in intuitive understanding. Some people find that sacred objects and tools help them tap into their inner reserves. Others are not inclined to use them at all. The most important part of intuition is our inner connection to the divine. That should always be our primary focus. All other things are only facilitators to the process.

Solution: If you are working well without objects, that's great. Don't feel the need to work with anything you aren't entirely comfortable with.

I ask you to look both ways. For the road to a knowledge of the stars leads through the atom; and important knowledge of the atom has been reached through the stars.

—Sir Arthur Eddington, Stars and Atoms (1928), Lecture

CHAPTER 18

ORACLES AND SACRED TOOLS: *Astrology, Numerology, Palmistry, I Ching, and Cards*

Oracles and sacred tools are metaphysical systems of learning that we can employ to assist in understanding ourselves or our life situations. Systems such as astrology, Tarot, I Ching, runes, palmistry, and numerology can be used as an interpretive foundation and source of guidance for our intuition. They also can provide external validation of our intuition, both for ourselves and for others. Ideally, they should be used in conjunction with, and in service to, our intuition and higher self. In this way, they can facilitate message work and readings, as well as provide deeper insights into our specific intuitive impressions.

Metaphysical systems, such as astrology, help us to discover our inner nature and how we relate to the world around us. Oracles can help us to understand the deeper psychospiritual trends that are manifesting as events, people, and situations in our daily lives. Throughout history, humankind has discovered many, many ways to systematically tap into our divine connection.

Nevertheless, if we are not careful and cognizant of our motivations, we can develop a dependency on our tools that can interfere with the intuitive process and, in the worst cases, also interfere with our own spiritual growth. If we allow our tools to speak too much for themselves, or treat them as a crutch for the intuitive process, we are only doing our higher selves a disservice. As long as we look to our tools in a spirit of nonreliance and liberation, we can find many productive and inspiring ways for them to assist us on our journey of spiritual discovery.

The following sections briefly outline some of the various metaphysical systems that we may employ to assist in our spiritual development. Each of us will be attracted to different methodologies, depending on our backgrounds and sensitivities. We should use the tools with which we feel most comfortable. We may choose to use one tool, or all of the tools, or none of them. If we are comfortable working with our intuition alone, then we should not feel a necessity to adopt a tool. However, if we choose to expand our psychic processes in this way, we may consider educating ourselves in some of the following subjects.

Metaphysical Systems

The following metaphysical systems have developed over the centuries, and each can offer very unique and insightful understanding of our world. These systems are based on the notion that there is a meaningful order, connectedness, and rhythm to all things. Astrology offers us an understanding of how the macrocosm unites with the microcosm through celestial movement. Numerology brings profound meaning to mathematics and numeric patterns. Palmistry illustrates how the physical body is a reflection of our spiritual choices and destinies. Knowledge of any of these systems will deepen our understanding of the meaningful nature of life.

Astrology

Historically speaking, astrology has been one of the most sublime metaphysical systems to grace humanity. It offers both a scientific and spiritual approach to self-discovery. The type of validation that astrology offers us is virtually unparalleled in this world. Not only is it a vehicle for self-mastery and evolution, but it also offers us tangible validation of our choices, our attitudes, and our life paths. It speaks directly to both our intuitive, faith-loving nature and our practical, evidence-seeking nature.

Astrology, as we know it in the West, is commonly understood to have originated in Mesopotamia around 4000 B.C. Astrology originally existed as a spiritual counterpart to its scientific co-system, astronomy. Systems of astrological/astronomical interpretation have also been documented in the Far East, as well as in the Americas as early as 5000 B.C. Over time, astrology and astronomy parted ways, one becoming a science, the other a spiritual art. The scientific age cast astrology into a dubious light, and it was often debunked as the work of charlatans, who created a prejudice toward the profound and insightful system that they abused. Today, the sublime and spiritual nature of astrology is at last being redeemed. Advances in physics, and the Theory of Relativity, have made a scientific explanation of this art feasible once again. As a consequence, astrology is now more readily embraced by the educated and higher-minded subsets of our culture.

We understand astrology as the manifestation of our spiritual blueprints, of the karma and dharma that we are committed to in this life. We all live amidst this cosmic tide of heavenly vibration, which is constantly interfacing with our own unique soul vibration. This "music of the spheres" pours through us with energies that touch our souls, as if they are the silent songs of the Heavens. Some songs will inspire us; some songs will keep us to ourselves; some songs will motivate us; some songs may be full of melancholy.

The celestial bodies, in this way, serve as God's messengers, as the physical manifestation of God's "word." The vibrations the planets emit during their cosmic parade imperceptibly link with our own physiology. More scientific approaches understand astrology as the interaction of microparticles and energy that invisibly fill our universe. In this view, astrology connects our world and our physical organisms with the vast cosmos, uniting the microcosm and macrocosm. Regardless of whether we attribute a spiritual or scientific explanation to astrological phenomenon, the process remains the same. Anyone who makes a sincere effort to understand astrology will, no doubt, gain valuable insights into his or her own life and the ways of the world.

The most important gift that we can receive from astrological understanding is the gift of self-understanding and, ultimately, self-mastery. It is an invaluable tool for getting in touch with our higher selves. We gain awareness of our natural affinities and disaffinities and learn the best ways to direct our energy in this world. We use our free will to manifest the higher aspects of our personality blueprint; we rise above ourselves to combat transient emotional and psychological challenges. Astrology enables us to be aware of the trends and cycles that form the tides of our lives. How we choose to navigate through the waters is up to us.

Because astrology is a science, it is possible to systematically interpret astrological aspects without the use of our intuition, if we have access to high-quality interpretive manuals. Nonetheless, we can look to the birth chart, as well as the planetary progressions and transits, as a source for intuitive inspiration as well as validations for the intuitive impressions that we receive.

Astrological symbols and house/aspect interpretations can

also become a strong foundation in our intuitive language with the Heavens. For example, if we are receiving psychic impressions regarding another person, Heaven may provide us with astrological information to help with our intuitive understanding of the situations in the person's life. We may receive clairvoyant impressions of planetary symbols or zodiac signs, each of which can serve as a profound point of intuitive departure for deeper elements of a message.

Regardless of whether or not we choose to utilize astrology as an active tool in our intuitive practices, such as formulating birth charts and horoscopes for ourselves and others, an understanding of astrology can deeply enrich our spiritual life and contribute to the effectiveness of our intuitive processes.

Numerology

The mystery of numbers is often underestimated. Mathematics can often be a daunting subject, particularly because the science of numbers and equations and problem-solving naturally lends itself to rigid-minded thinking. The well-known Greek mathematician Pythagoras established a system of understanding the meaningful nature of numbers around 500 B.C. This system is still in widespread use today. But the origins of numerology extend much farther into history, as far back as the Hebrew Kabbalah. Throughout history, spiritual seekers have understood that numerology can allow us to see the depth, the mystery, the profundity in the mathematical process. Numerology gives *meaning* to numbers.

The numbers that function within our lives, particularly through our date of birth and the numbers associated with our name, can be valuable indicators of the kinds of vibrations that we are working with in our lives. Each number contains within it a distinct vibration; each number is one unique unit. Together, they add up to the universal whole. Each letter of the alphabet also carries with it a numeric value that equates to a similar cosmic vibration. The expression of these numbers and letters in our life can paint a numerological portrait of our soul's purpose, and can assist us in the understanding of our character, our talents, and our relationships.

An understanding of numerology, like astrology, can be beneficial to our intuitive development. When we gain an intuitive understanding of the vibrations of each number, we can extend that intuitive understanding to situations and individuals we encounter in our lives. Heaven may also use numbers, and their vibrations, as components of our intuitive language. For example, we may intuitively sense a number 4 vibration around someone, or even have clairvoyant or clairaudient impressions of the number 4. We then may begin to sense that the characteristics of a number 4 vibration, like stability, security, or conservatism, may be a dominant issue in that person's life. Numbers, like any other symbol, can be an excellent point of departure for psychic understanding.

Numerology is yet another path to understanding that can assist us in our life choices. It is consistent with other metaphysical systems such as astrology. Ideally, an understanding of these systems will complement each other as much as it enriches our lives.

Palmistry

If we understand the meaningful nature of everything in life, we may begin to understand how our human physiology is a direct manifestation of our soul and life purpose. Every aspect of our body is information about ourselves on a deeper level, whether it is being expressed through our overall health, our genetics, or even through the most minute markings, especially on the hand.

Palmistry is based on the notion that the details of our hands are a manifestation of our thoughts and life path, both conscious and subconscious. Each person's hands have a unique shape and size, as well as a unique pattern of lines upon the palms and fingertips. Law enforcement has utilized fingerprinting for the past 100 years as a source of identification, because each of us has a unique fingerprint. Palmists suggest that this uniqueness is more than a random biological phenomenon. Fingerprinting has been used in India and China for centuries as a means of psychological and physiological understanding. Recent medical research has documented correspondences between genetic abnormalities and distinctive markings on the hands, as well as the hand shape and size. Scientists have postulated that hormonal conditions in utero may be a link that connects initial hand formation with propensities to certain chronic illnesses.

In palmistry, the body and mind are seen as a symbiotic unit, perpetually interconnected in the process of self-expression. Our hands are the part of the body that is most intimately connected with our self-expression. Whether we are writing, painting, playing musical instruments, building, touching, or even driving, our hands are a crucial factor in how we express our personal energy into the world. They are our primary medium for connecting our inner workings to our external reality. Thus, it is an apt suggestion that our hands would, in some way, be a reflection of the energy that is constantly passing through them. The lines on the hand have been compared to ripples in the water, resonating with the electromagnetic thought-energy that flows through the palms.

Some of the most insightful intuitives in history have utilized palmistry as a tool for psychic awareness. Hand information can present us with a plethora of intuitive points of departure. Most often, we recognize distinctive hand traits that point to general issues, then rely on our intuition to extrapolate the specific details. Contrary to popular belief, the lines on our hands do not predict our fate. Our free will can always change a prophecy. Palmistry, like any other psychic tool, can only point us in the direction of our potential.

Oracles

Oracles have been used throughout history as a means of divination. The ancients learned that it was possible to work with these oracles in order to gain a deeper understanding of the unseen forces. Unfortunately, many oracles have gained a rather taboo reputation over the centuries because of abuse by their practitioners. As with anything else on this earth, the integrity of the oracle only goes as far as the integrity of its user. These oracles can be a profound source of inner guidance and understanding, if we choose to use them wisely.

I Ching

This ancient sacred text, also known as the Book of Changes, is one of civilization's oldest forms of divination. Originating more than 3,000 years ago in the East as a part of Confucianism, it has since become one of the most popular spiritual resources in Asia, and has become an increasingly well known part of Western spiritualist culture.

The I Ching is a complex and deeply spiritual system of personal enlightenment, and is profoundly connected with Taoist and Zen Buddhist philosophy. Instead of using card formations and patterns to convey symbolic or metaphoric messages, the I Ching bases its interpretation upon the relationships among coins or sticks that are tossed, then examined based on the yin/yang principle. This principle represents the constant change and motion of the universe, as well as that of our lives. As we understand our life experience in terms of this interplay, we begin to better understand our course.

Though everyday use of the I Ching is generally complemented by the interpretation the book itself includes, we can use the I Ching to assist in our intuition as we ponder the relationships expressed in the principle of yin and yang. The feelings and impressions associated with the various hexagrams can carry over into our intuitive language and provide us with insights into the nature of the action or inaction that Heaven may be calling for.

Runes

The runes have been called the I Ching of the Vikings. Older than the New Testament, this ancient alphabet and divination tool was a significant cultural element in the Scandinavian areas of Sweden, Norway, Denmark, Iceland, and northern Germany, and extended into the British Isles and even remote parts of North America. Use of the runes spanned from the mundane, as a form of writing, to the sublime, as a form of divination.

Every rune is associated with unique esoteric meanings and translates into a word or phrase symbolic of concepts that reflect the human condition. Many of the ancient secrets of the runes have been lost, because the keepers of the Runic wisdom and traditions, the rune masters, were forced into seclusion with the rise of medieval Christianity.

The runes, as an oracle, are created by carving or painting the runic letters upon stones, clay, or any other appropriate surface. Each stone has one letter, which serves as a symbol for a general interpretive theme. The stones, when cast into specific spreads, represent the psychospiritual dynamics that surround a situation or life, much like the Tarot or the I Ching.

This unique and ancient tool can assist our intuition with our understanding of its symbology. Like the other tools, this one enriches our intuitive vocabulary and strengthens our interpretive abilities.

Cards

Probably the most popular oracle among recent generations is the card deck. There is a card deck to suit every individual, from unique contemporary decks, such as the Angel cards, to traditional or modernized versions of the Tarot. Each deck is usually composed of 78 cards. This system of divination is often used to clarify life circumstances, to understand trends of unfolding events, and to develop psychic ability through spiritual awareness.

When we work with the cards, we are essentially working with our higher selves. The power of card reading lies not in the cards themselves, but in our own minds and spirits. Through the shuffling and meditative processes, we unconsciously arrange the cards into an order that will reflect the deeper spiritual nature of the events and trends in our lives. In this way, the cards serve as a link between our conscious minds and our higher selves. They provide us with deeper insight into the meaning of our choices and the consequences of their outcomes.

A popular misunderstanding surrounding card reading, especially the Tarot, is that in order to use the cards, we must memorize each one's unique meaning, a task that would require an immense amount of work and intelligence. Decks like the Tarot are created on principles of symbology and metaphor that are designed to enliven our imagination and intuition, in order that we might find our own meaning and understanding of each card. We view each card as a symbolic scene, one that may speak to us differently each time that it is drawn. We may focus on different aspects of the same card at different times, therefore bringing a unique depth to each interpretation. Our higher self draws us to the pertinent aspects of each symbol and each card scenario, which then serve as our point of intuitive departure for further meaning.

In this way, more than any other tool, the cards can play a valuable role in our intuitive development. As we learn their symbology, we stimulate and develop our intuitive language. We become more adept at the intuitive process by regularly practicing this manner of interpretation. Even if we never choose to use the cards in professional readings or for our message work with others, they can be an excellent vehicle for informal psychic practice as well as for insight into the workings of our own intuitive process.

Card Reading Workshop

Using Card Decks as a Source of Intuitive Understanding

Card decks can be one of the most useful tools for assisting the intuitive process. They can help us strengthen our intuitive visual language through their symbols and imagery, as well as provide us with tangible points of intuitive departure. It may be helpful for a beginner to read a reference manual to gain a general understanding of the subtleties of each card, but after that it is not necessary to use a manual at all. Most individuals who work intimately with cards do not use a manual for interpretation and have not memorized the elaborate, specific meanings that such references describe for each card. Instead, card readers work with the symbols, images, colors, and numbers on each card as points of departure for unique interpretations for each card, and each individual they read for.

Our cards can mean whatever they mean to us. They may seem to mean one thing at a certain point, then another thing at another point, depending on the nature of the reading. For example, if we are working with a card that depicts a man on a horse riding into the sunset, our interpretation of that card will depend on what aspect of the image our attention is drawn to. If we look at the card and find ourselves immediately focusing on the horse, we might get the impression that travel will become an issue for the person being read for. Our intuition can continue on from that point, perhaps offering us more insight as to the destination or reason for the journey. On the other hand, the next time the same card shows up in a reading, we may be drawn to an entirely different aspect of it. Instead of the horse, we may find ourselves focusing on the sunset. We may get the impression that a literal or symbolic journey is coming to an end, that the "sun is setting" on a particular aspect of the individual's life. Again, our intuition can provide us with more information based on this point of departure.

Learning to understand the cards is largely the process of learning to communicate through metaphor and symbolism. We recognize a metaphorical situation and apply it to our lives, or the lives of those we are reading for. We may find ourselves speaking in parables, or even in riddles. Direct answers or commands are rarely given. Heaven wants to help us on our path, but does not want to give us all the answers. Heaven, like a good schoolteacher, will guide us, inspire us, and help us to understand our problems, but will not do our work for us. We must choose our own actions and our own future if our success is to be our own.

To begin working with the cards, find a deck that suits you. The Tarot is the most popular of all card decks, with hundreds of different styles to choose from. Find a deck with imagery that appeals to your sensibilities, ideally one rich in illustrative content. The more information on each card, the more information for your intuition to use as points of departure. If you prefer to use a deck other than the Tarot, the same advice applies. The key is to find one deck that you are comfortable with and that provides you with a source of intuitive inspiration. When you find that deck, continue to use it until you become thoroughly familiar with it. The more familiar you become with a deck, the easier it will be to recognize the different energies that each card signifies. Get to know your deck by working with it for readings for yourself, or simply by contemplating the cards one by one. This will allow you to become intimate with the deck and familiar with the way each card speaks to you.

The following spreads are examples of different ways that we can use the cards to assist our intuitive development and to seek divine guidance for ourselves or others. You may use any type of card deck during this type of intuitive work; use the deck that you feel most comfortable with. Before each session with the cards, you should be sure to recharge them with your energy, usually by shuffling them as you quiet your mind and center yourself. Concentrate on any pertinent issues at hand, as well as receiving information in the divine spirit of love and wisdom.

Daily Card Messages

Choosing a daily message card is a great way to get familiar with your deck and with how your intuition works with your cards. Each morning, when your day is fresh, select a random card from your deck. This card will be a significator for some aspect of your upcoming day. It could indicate your mood for the day, or events or people who will influence you.

In the beginning, you may just want to make note of the card and watch how its energy manifests throughout the day. Eventually, you may become so familiar with the cards that you will begin to understand what trends or kinds of events may be waiting to manifest before they actually occur.

You can also use this system for daily guidance from your cards. When you are about to choose your card, ask Heaven what message you should keep in mind for your upcoming day. If, for example, you pull the Temperance card, you may want to prepare yourself to exercise patience and calmness toward any unforeseen situations. You also can do some "intuitive brainstorming" to gain any additional insights from your chosen card. Keeping a daily journal of your card messages and their manifestations can help you to keep track of the intuitive system that you are building.

Card Spreads

When you begin to use the cards for guidance on specific life issues, for yourself or for others, you will find an endless variety of card layout systems to assist in this process. Choose whatever spreads work best for you. Each person will prefer to work with different spreads, depending on his or her sensibilities and the subject matter involved.

This workshop will illustrate some basic spreads that can assist our intuitive process.

Tips

- Always pay close attention to any cards that fall from the deck during the shuffling process. Generally, these cards reveal themselves for a reason. Often they will show up in the spread or will validate an intuition for you. Cards that "jump" from the deck are often the most important cards in a reading. They are the cards Heaven can't resist showing you, the ones it doesn't want you to overlook.
- Decide how you interpret reversed cards. In a spread, some cards will appear in the upright position, and others will be upside down. You may choose to simply turn all of the

cards into their upright position, and disregard any reversals. The other option is to view reversals as a statement about the energy flow around each card's subject matter. In this case, upright cards are considered to manifest a positive flow of their energy; reversed cards are generally thought to symbolize a blocked energy flow, or circumstances that are not ready to happen just yet.

- Use your intuition to determine when the shuffle is complete. Continue shuffling until you feel a sense that you are done, or until you instinctively lay the cards down. Whenever you think that you are finished with the shuffle, you are.
- Remember, no card that you receive regarding future events implies a one-and-only outcome. It represents the probable outcome—if our thought process continue as they are. If you don't like the card in a Future position, you should rethink your approach to the situation that is leading you there.

Preparation

Before you begin working with the cards, find a quiet place where you will not be interrupted. You may wish to meditate, or add any ambiance that contributes to your inner calm, like lighting a candle or using incense. Shuffle the cards extensively before each use, until you feel that you have saturated them with your energy and given them a new mix. While you are shuffling your cards, concentrate on the specific issues for which you will be receiving guidance. As you prepare to lay out your cards, ask your question as specifically as possible, in order to have the least amount of ambiguity in the reading.

Rainbow Spread: Past, Present, and Future

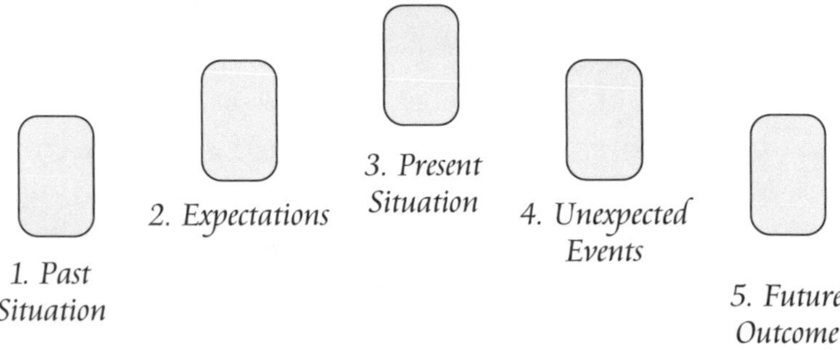

This spread is an excellent way to understand trends of any specific situation that you are amid, as well as general themes in your life. This spread represents the energy flow around the specific situation, based on the current choices of action.

1. To begin, shuffle the cards and then lay them face-up in the shape of a rainbow.
2. Start with the Past card and end with the Future card.
3. Ask Heaven for guidance according to the highest possible good. In some instances, you may choose to specify the length of time involved, for clarity's sake. Then work with your intuition to interpret the symbolism and meaning that each card represents.

Interpretation

Past situation: This card provides you with insights regarding the nature of the energies that caused the situation to originate. This is the why, when, and how of the original purpose of the situation. The Past card can help you to become aware of unconscious thoughts that have attracted you to become involved in the situation at hand.

Expectations: This card indicates your conscious expectations surrounding the situation. It can indicate your motivations, or what you think you should achieve or gain from the situation. But what we expect is often an illusion that we create in order to fulfill our ego drives. This card can make you aware of the true nature of the motivations that have led the situation to its current status.

Present situation: This card symbolizes the current situation—the general meaning of the current events and perspectives. It helps you to understand why you are in the place that you are, and how your choices have manifested in your present life.

Unexpected events: This card will indicate any unforeseen events or changes that are going to affect the situation. It can represent the turning point of the situation, or any forks in the road. In any case, it indicates how you should expect the unexpected, and allow those forces to transform the situation for the best of all involved.

Future outcome: This card provides you with clues as to how current thought patterns and choices, in tandem with any unexpected change, will manifest as future outcomes. This is how your will unites with Heaven's will, if your choices continue on the present track. If you change your approach to the situation, a new outcome is always possible.

Two Paths: The Decision-Making Spread

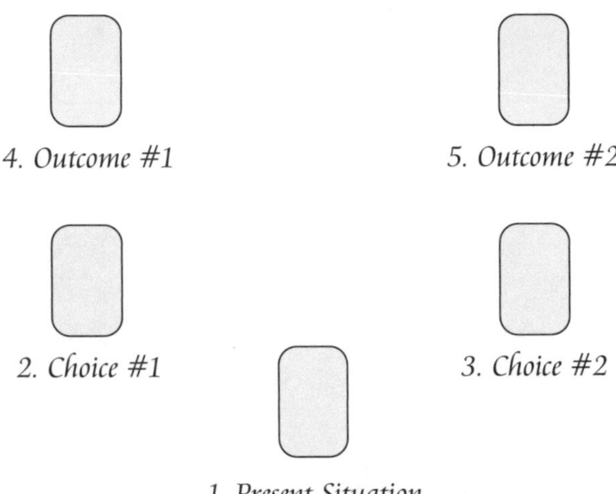

This is an excellent spread for guidance with decision-making. It deals with the outcomes of your situation based on two separate paths of action (although you could draw a spread for three or four different outcomes, should that ever be necessary).

1. To begin, shuffle the cards as you concentrate on the situation at hand.
2. When the shuffle is complete, lay out the cards face-up, starting with the Present Situation card. Continue with the Choice #1 card, then the Choice #2 card. Finish with the Outcome #1 card, and finally the Outcome #2 card.
3. As always, ask Heaven for guidance in the highest possible good. Then allow your intuition to connect meaning to the cards and their placements.

Interpretation

Present situation: This card signifies the overall situation and the energy surrounding the present circumstances. This card can point you to the higher awareness or transformation that events are leading you to.

Choice #1: This card indicates circumstances that are pulling you toward Outcome #1. These are the forces that you are being called to choose or to reject.

Choice #2: This card indicates circumstances that are pulling you toward Outcome #2. These are the other forces that you are being called to choose or to reject.

Outcome #1: This card suggests the probable outcome to the situation, if you engage the energy of the Choice #1 card.

Outcome #2: This card suggests the probable outcome to the situation, if you engage the energy of the Choice #2 card.

With the spread complete, you can get an overall feeling for the situation, and each potential outcome. Your intuition will guide you through the interpretation.

The Star: Self-Awareness Spread

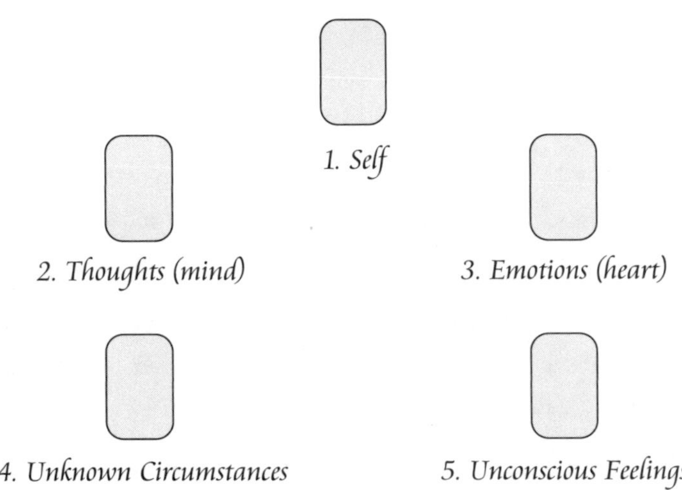

The Star is the ideal spread to help you understand the nature of your thoughts and feelings toward particular people or situations in your life. We often find ourselves in the midst of complicated relationships or circumstances, for reasons that we are not always fully aware of. This spread can help you to become more conscious of our lessons and motivations for creating these scenarios in our lives. Like a star, this spread can bring much illumination to the dark places in your life.

1. To begin, shuffle the cards and then lay them out while concentrating on the issues at hand.
2. Begin by pulling the Self card, and then work your way down to the Unconscious Feelings card, from left to right.
3. Once all the cards are drawn, quiet your mind and allow your intuition to flow.

Interpretation

Self: This card is the overall significator of your self in the current situation. It provides you with insight into the general overall meaning of your role in the situation, as well as any lessons or tests that you are enduring.

Thoughts: This card represents your conscious approach to the situation or person. This is how you think about them, or how your rational approach to the situation is manifesting.

Emotions: This card represents your emotional approach to the situation or person. This is how you feel about them, or how your emotions are affecting the circumstances.

Unknown circumstances: This card represents the external circumstances surrounding the situation that elude your awareness. They may be secrets. They may be things that are being withheld from you. They may also be things that you simply fail to notice for lack of attention. At any rate, this card will indicate any crucial factors that you may not be aware of.

Unconscious feelings: This card represents the internal feelings and habit patterns surrounding the situation that elude your awareness. They may be unconscious defense mechanisms, or insecurities, or habits formed so long ago that they seem to be a part of your personality. This card points you to any issues within yourself that require your awareness and re-evaluation. You must address these issues in order to fully understand the situation at hand, and how to grow through it.

Once you have gained an understanding of the meaning that each of these cards holds for your situation, take a few moments to meditate on how you can use this awareness to better understand yourself and express yourself in the situation at hand.

The Arrow: Current Life Direction Spread

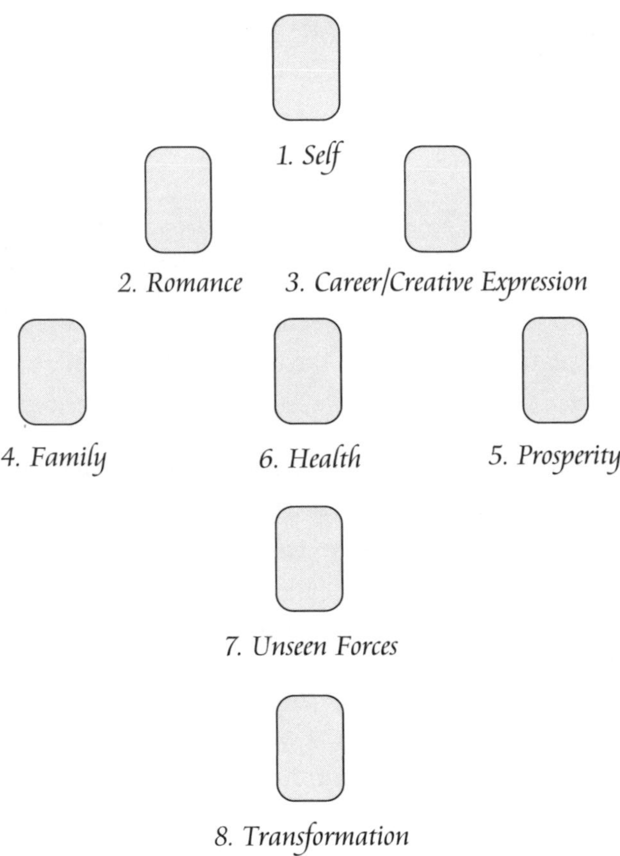

This is perhaps the most complex card spread, but it is also the most comprehensive for getting an overall feel for a person's current position in life. This spread is like a "snapshot" of things as they are at the moment. This spread is most beneficial when you are reading for other people, though it can be a useful tool for your personal growth as well. It deals with the various aspects of our lives and also provides a visual diagram of the direction in which our current choices are taking us.

We can understand the arrow as an illustration of all of the different forces within our lives that point to the current state of our "self." The left side of the arrow represents the manifestation of our inner "yin" resources, such as love, affection, family, and togetherness. The right side of the arrow represents the manifestation of our external "yang" resources, such as creativity, success, prosperity, and individuality. The Health card stands in the middle as a symbolic measure of how well we are integrating the left and right sides of the arrow into our lives.

1. Shuffle the cards while focusing on your subject.
2. Lay them out, face-up, starting with the Self card and finishing with the Transformation card.
3. Ask for guidance in the spirit of the highest good for everyone involved in the situation. Then allow your intuition to attach insight to the cards.

Interpretation

Self: Again, this card is the overall significator of the self at the current life moment. It reveals to us the energy that is dominant in our life at this time, as well as the primary lessons we are involved with.

Romance: This card indicates the way in which love and romance are integrated into our life. This card specifically refers to romantic partnerships or marriages, or lack thereof. The most important message this card reveals is how we are able to share ourselves with others, on an intimate, one-on-one basis.

Career/creative expression: This card reveals the way we are manifesting our creative drives in the world. This may be through career, or talents, or any interests that involve directing our personal energies externally for our own self-expression or success.

Family: This card indicates the way in which we express ourselves in the family environment. Depending on the person, this card could represent circumstances with our parents, children, brothers and sisters, or even extended family. The most important message this card reveals is how we are able to support and/or are supported by the group structure of loved ones in our lives.

Prosperity: This card reveals how we are creating prosperity in our lives—how our self-expression and motivation has manifested into wealth, power, wisdom, or material comforts.

Health: This card indicates the kind of energy that is directly affecting any health issues. It can make us aware of what energy needs to be balanced in order to live in an optimum state of physical, mental, and emotional health.

Unseen forces: This card indicates forces that are at work below the surface of the current life situation. These are the forces that call us to change, to become more aware, or to grow into a new life. The more we resist these forces, the more out of balance the previously discussed dimensions of our lives will become. The more that we accept and flow with the changes, the more self-actualized we become.

Transformation: This card is the root of all the other cards in the spread. Its energy signifies the propulsive force that is fueling the overall life situation. This card represents the higher meaning of the trials and tribulations that we currently are experiencing. The energy of this card fuels the Unseen Forces, which, in turn, influence the rest of the spread. When we understand how we are being called to transform our selves, we can then get a better understanding of how we can work with the underlying forces of change in our life.

Future Events Spread

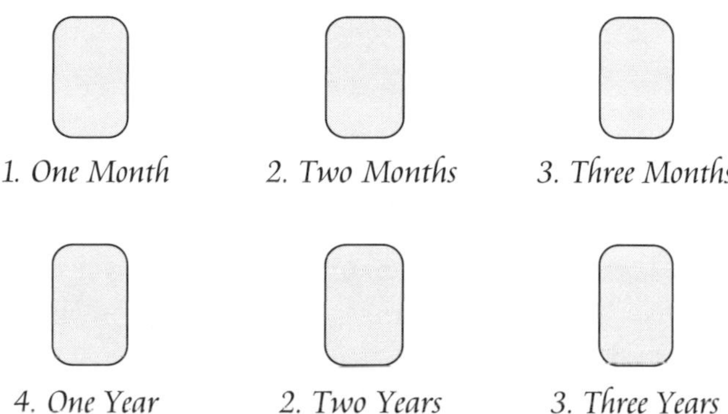

This spread can help you to understand the trends of life events that may be coming your way. Since all future events depend on the choices of your free will, the manifestation of these events depends upon your continuing on your current path. Many less desirable circumstances can be avoided by changing your patterns of choice, as well as your manner of approaching the situation at hand.

The time frames used in the spread above can be modified to suit any inquiry. The top row is set up as the short-term future; the bottom row represents the long-term future.

1. Shuffle the cards and lay them out while concentrating on a specific issue.
2. Lay out the cards face-up, left to right, beginning with the One Month card and ending with the Three Years card.
3. Allow your intuition to flow. Begin your interpretation.

Interpretation

One month: This card can provide insight into events and circumstances that are apt to manifest in the upcoming month.

Two months: This card deals with events and circumstances the following month.

Three months: This card deals with the same for the third month.

One year: This card provides insight into dominant themes or events that are apt to occur in the upcoming year.

Two years: This card deals with themes or events of the following year.

Three years: This card deals with the same for the third year.

Frequently Asked Questions

Question: "Can I create my own card spread?"

Explanation: There is no specific set way to use the cards. Most people choose to use some of the more popular spreads found in manuals or that come with the card decks. However, you are free to develop any system that works for you.

Solution: Be as creative as you like with your card spreads. Figure out what works for you; then practice it.

Question: "What do I do when I don't quite understand the meaning of a card?"

Explanation: It is not uncommon to occasionally find yourself a little stumped about the meaning of a card as it applies to a specific situation. If this is the case, tune in to your intuition the best that you can. If you get nothing, you can draw additional cards for clarification.

Solution: Develop a routine for drawing additional cards; then implement it consistently. You may choose to draw the next card from the top of the deck, sequentially, or you can choose random cards from the deck.

Question: "Why do the same cards seem to keep showing up over and over in my spreads?"

Explanation: This is how Heaven alerts you to consistent themes in your life. Recurring cards signify issues that you have not yet resolved, issues that persist in your sphere of experience. Also, cards sometimes recur to reinforce certain points to you and to serve as validations as you move in a certain direction.

Solution: Pay close attention to recurring cards. They are a clear indicator of trends in your life.

Solution: Try recording the cards you are working with in a journal, in order to keep track of patterns. It is interesting to see how often the same cards pop up when we are working with similar themes.

Question: "How often can I do readings for myself, or another person?"

Explanation: There is no specific length of time you should wait between readings. However, you should be careful not to overdo or abuse the process by using it too often. Your intuition will clue you in as to whether or not you are ready for another reading. If you don't feel good about the prospect of a reading, then it is probably too soon. Some people are comfortable doing mini-readings for themselves daily, while others may only wish to approach the cards once a month or even once a year, in order to receive an in-depth reading.

Solution: Let your intuition guide you as to the best time to seek or conduct a reading for yourself.

Summary

As you interpret the cards during your readings, pay attention to any specific intuitive impressions that may accompany each card. More specific details, feelings, or thoughts may come to you through your psychic senses. Supplemental reading on numerology, Tarot interpretation, or symbology may assist the interpretation process.

Reason is our soul's left hand, Faith her right,
By these we reach divinity.

—*John Donne (c. 1572–1631)*

CHAPTER 19

DEAD MAN TALKING: *Linking to Souls in Spirit Through Mediumship*

It is easy for us to forget, amidst the apparent silence of our "lost" loved ones, that they are still among us. Though we may be deprived of sharing life's little luxuries with them, we are never deprived of their presence in our lives. We may not be able to have dinner together anymore, or feel the comfort and warmth of our embraces with them, but we still have their guidance and their support on another level. It is always difficult when we lose the physical connection with those we love. Still, we can find comfort that our emotional, mental, and spiritual connection will endure endlessly.

The art of mediumship can assist us in strengthening the connections we still have with our loved ones in spirit. Mediumship can serve as our spiritual reminder—the little tap on the shoulder and the whispered "See, I am still with you."

Mediumship is one of the most publicized and popular

expressions of psychic ability in our contemporary culture. The media and general public are finally embracing the healing and life-affirming messages that mediumship can offer us, as individuals including John Edward, James Van Praagh, Sylvia Browne, and George Anderson have taken mediumship to new levels of public interest. By demystifying the mediumistic process, and by offering hope and peace to the bereaved, these mediums, along with countless others, are a testament to the healing power mediumship can offer.

Mediumship is a more controversial aspect of intuitive awareness because it generally involves direct communication with the "dead people" or other guides and spiritual teachers. While our intuition guides us and provides us with information and direction, mediumship allows us to experience, one on one, a personal connection with souls in the spiritual dimension. During this process, we are able to receive impressions through our intuition and the meta-senses directly from or in reference to particular spiritual beings. Most often, these beings are departed loved ones. In the afterlife, souls do not speak with words, but with thoughts. Thought is the medium of spiritual communication. Thoughts flow among us and through us in a ceaseless river, connecting all life in a stream of consciousness.

During this process, we feel a soul's presence psychically, through our meta-senses. Though the soul generally will not manifest in physical space, we still can communicate and interact with him or her much as we would with a person still in physical form. In fact, there is little difference in the time between us and them, aside from the fact that we have bodies and they do not. They joke with us. They laugh with us. They get excited with us. But most of all, they share with us. They have come to us to share with us the fact of their continued existence, despite the fact that most of us cannot see them, or feel them at all. They are still alive. They are still themselves. And they are still with us.

Receiving Mediumistic Impressions

We receive mediumistic impressions in the same way that we receive general intuitive impressions, through our intuition or meta-senses. The difference is that, with mediumship, we generally are working with a specific soul personality, or even groups of soul personalities, such as friends and family members who come together to communicate to us from the spiritual plane. We also often find ourselves dealing with information that is of a distinctly personal nature, so that only the sender of the information (the soul in spirit) and receiver (the person here on earth) know its true meaning. Even the simplest word or phrase can be a meaningful form of evidence for survival of the soul personality after death. When we bring information through in this way, we can help others to experience this continuous structure of life in a personal and life-changing way.

Souls may give us visual impressions so that we may describe their appearance, or even the appearance of objects or places that may come through for validation. They may give us auditory impressions, most commonly their names. We may get the sound of a full name, or sometimes only an initial or syllable, depending on the clarity of the channel of communication. They may also give us feelings as information, and oftentimes, these feelings are distinctly physical. We may actually feel pressure, heat, tingling, or muscle spasms in specific parts of our body. This is often to convey information about the spirits' health during life, or information regarding their passing.

As our intuitive language and our ability to receive and pass on information grow, we become more adept at working with souls no longer in a physical body. These souls communicate with us through assistance from our own spiritual teachers and guides, who are already intimately familiar with us and our intuitive language. In this way, souls may show us events from our own lives, as well as symbols we have become accustomed to, in order to communicate their own information.

 Mediumship Workshop

Connecting the Physical and Spiritual Realms

Most people do not realize that we are all natural mediums. As human beings, we stand between the two worlds, the world of the spirit and the world of the flesh. We have a dual nature implicit in our very existence. This duality allows us to function on both the material and spiritual planes, though our physical existence is more tangible to our perception. When we learn how to understand our more subtle spiritual existence, we can reach profound new levels of awareness.

When we decide to embrace our natural mediumistic abilities, we should understand our role as the "medium" between the realm of energy and the realm of matter, thought, and form. Just as the artist works with paint, or ink, or clay as a medium for self-expression, Heaven can work with us as a living medium of divine expression. Through us, through our minds and bodies, Heaven can manifest its word.

The following workshop is divided into two sections. The first describes how to use mediumship to bring other people together with their departed loved ones; the second describes how to use our mediumship ability to connect with our own loved ones on the other side. Though the process is the same for both, there is a distinct difference between the two. The work we do for others remains objective, as long as we don't already know too much about the lives of the people we are dealing with. However, the work we do for ourselves always has to battle the subjectivity of our memory and past personal experiences with our loved ones.

Tips

Below are helpful tips for what you can expect when communicating with souls:

- There are two primary reasons souls choose to communicate transdimensionally: to let their loved ones know that they have not actually died at all—that they are alive and all right; and to remind those loved ones of their continued love and presence in their lives. Almost all messages and information that you receive will revolve around one of these two notions.
- Souls will give you personal, private information to confirm to their loved ones that they are truly present. Seemingly meaningless information can be the most profound validation of the presence of a loved one.
- It is not unusual for souls to make jokes, reminisce, or offer their advice or even hints about upcoming big events.
- Often, you will get distinct impressions of people, just as if you were meeting them in everyday life. You can sense a soul's personality, as well as any details of former physical appearance that he or she chooses to show you. Because they are living energy, souls are not confined to a permanent physical form, as we are; however, they generally choose to manifest to us the details of the former physical body. This is the way that their loved ones would be most likely to recognize them.
- Souls on the other side are often as new to this process as you may be. They may not know the best way to proceed, with good psychic manners, or they may be overwhelmed to witness the process working. They become accustomed to not being heard, or seen, or felt, except in subtle ways, so when at last a person recognizes them consciously, it can

be as exciting for them as it is for the people in the physical world. The process often is a reunion. Even though our souls are never truly far from the ones we love in spirit, it can seem that a million miles and an eternity stand between us when the lines of communication are down. Mediumship is a process of reconnecting the power lines between the physical and spiritual planes of existence, of disintegrating the illusory distance between us and them.

- You must be particularly regimented in your centering and self-protection rituals when you work with mediumship. When you open your self during this process, you open yourself directly to energy from souls in spirit. You always want to have the ability to receive or not to receive that energy at your will. If you work without proper preparation, your sensitivity can affect you detrimentally. Practice meditation both before and after working as a medium.

Mediumship and the Loved Ones of Others

We begin to work with mediumship in the same way that we work with any of our other intuitive functions. We establish a peaceful environment, then spend some time centering, protecting and, ultimately, opening our selves to the heavenly energies. We also may choose to work more consciously with our spiritual guides, or guardians, during this process. These souls will function as our gatekeepers as we work with our intuition to interface with the various souls who wish to communicate with us. As we are preparing ourselves to do so, we can ask our primary guide, the one we are most familiar with, to gather and prepare any souls in the spiritual realm who hope to connect with us. Our guide can help the process to flow smoothly, to let each soul come through, one by one, thus avoiding the chaos of one soul trying to push through over another in order to be heard.

We can work with groups, or specific individuals, or even alone. We generally have little control over who comes through to us. Heaven will bring the souls to us according to its own reason. The spirit world knows who is available to receive messages; though we may want to connect with specific people in spirit, it is up to Heaven to decide whether or not that happens. We should be open to anyone who comes through to us, and not look for specific souls to connect to.

Once we establish a connection with a soul in spirit, we can proceed with them as we would any other human being. We can ask them questions (which may or may not be answered), laugh with them, and talk with them. They will reveal to us only the information that we need to know, or only the information they want us to know. We can persist with our questions, but if we are not meant to know their answers, Heaven will not reveal them to us. Heaven is never to interfere with issues that may affect our free will or violate our privacy.

Before we begin a mediumship session, we should take a moment to express our intention to work as a messenger between the physical and spiritual realms, and to ask our guides to prepare us as well as anyone on the other side who may wish to connect with us. Once we are centered, and in our quiet meditative state, we are ready to begin.

Mediumship Using the Three-Step Intuitive Process

1. **Stimulus:** Affirm to yourself, and your spiritual guardians, that you are ready to connect with any souls in spirit who wish to communicate with those in the physical world. Ask that, at Heaven's will, the souls be allowed to touch in with you, one by one. Take a moment to extend a mental welcome to the souls whom you are about to meet.

2. **Response:** Open your intuitive mind to any impressions

you may start to receive. The process will work differently for different people. Some people have an immediate awareness of a soul's presence around them. Some people will hear distinct voices. Some will clairvoyantly "see" the souls who are touching in with them. Some will get distinct feelings about the personality and events around the soul. Most often, you will experience a combination of these things, in your own specific way. Your guide will probably use a consistent system, so pay attention and learn your own unique rhythm as the process unfolds for you.

3. **Synthesis:** Focus on the impressions you receive from the soul, and begin to interact with him or her. You can ask questions regarding the soul's name, appearance, the reason for his or her transition to the spirit world, or anything that might help you validate the soul's presence to loved ones.

Examples of Mediumistic Impressions

PHYSICAL APPEARANCE

The first thing that many souls will choose to show us is an impression of their former physical appearance. This allows us to describe the person to his or her loved ones in the physical world, and is an excellent way for souls to identify themselves.

> **Example:** You may "see" the impression of gray hair pulled back in a bun. From that, you will probably ascertain that the soul lived to an older age, and was female. More details may fall into place, like the way she dressed, or things that people often saw her doing, like cooking, or canning fruit. You may even start to receive details about the way her house looked, as well as any furniture or household items that would be associated with her. Depending on the soul's nature and interests in life, this sort of thing could go in any direction. Go wherever you are led.

NAME

During a meduimistic session you are likely to have letters, words, or portions of words pop into your mind, particularly if you have asked the soul for his or her name. Some people find it very easy to get the names of the souls who come through to them, while others may never get one. Don't be frustrated if you fall into the latter category. It just means who you are getting your strongest information through meta-senses other than clairaudience.

> **Example:** Often you will get a phonetic sound, or series of sounds, that constitutes part of the name. For example, if the soul's name was James, you may get the impression of a "J" or a "JM" or combination thereof, so you put the pieces together to form a "James" or "Jim" or "Jamie." Often this process, combined with the help of the loved ones who are hoping to communicate with the soul, allows us to put a name with the soul.

> **Example:** Souls will often employ the other psychic senses to reveal their names. For example, if you receive an impression of Marlene Dietrich, you should consider asking the person you are working with if he or she has anyone in spirit by the name of Marlene. Similarly, if you keep getting impressions of daisies, you may want to ask if the name Daisy has any significance to anyone.

DATE

Souls will often identify themselves by significant dates, or may want to recognize the date (often either the month or the day, not usually both) of important events. In the former, they may give the date of their birth (even their zodiac sign), the date of their transition, or the dates of any important anniversaries. In the latter, they may give the date of the person's birthday, or the birthday of any of their immediate loved ones, or any other significant dates in their lives.

> **Example:** You may get impressions of numbers that correspond to months ("1" being January, "2" being February, and so forth) or to the days of the month ("28"). You may get impressions of the seasons as clarification. Sometimes you may even be required to do mathematics; Heaven has been known to show us the number 4 by showing us the number 2 twice. So, discount nothing until you understand how the process works for you. You will undoubtedly have your own unique approach to all the intuitive information you receive.

CAUSE OF TRANSITION TO THE SPIRIT REALM

There are many ways for souls to express to us the reason for their passing. Some souls do not wish to deal with this at all, for it can be, surprisingly enough, a sensitive subject, particularly if there is any tension or self-consciousness surrounding the manner of transition. But most souls are not reluctant to tell us how they "died."

> **Example:** One common way to sense the cause for transition is through clairsentience. Souls can impress upon us feelings or sensations that help us to understand the location or nature of the cause of bodily death. For example, a pain or sensation in the chest could point to heart-related issues. A feeling of vertigo, or dizziness, could indicate alcohol- or drug-related issues. These feelings are generally distinct, but should never be painful or overwhelm you. They are given to us momentarily as information only, and should dissipate in no time at all.

Example: Another way that souls can communicate their cause of transition is by showing us the parts of the body that were affected at the time of death. Often, if we are able to see them clairvoyantly, they will actually show us where a sickness or injury occurred by pointing out a particular part of the body. For example, if a soul is pointing to the head, this may indicate a head injury, or even a stroke or brain tumor. Ask for more information if you need clarification.

Really, souls will use any means necessary to convey this information. They may give you the impression of someone else you knew who died the same way. They may give you symbols, or even draw you pictures.

Personal Information

You will need to rely on your five meta-senses to bring through the many kinds of personal information that souls will attempt to pass on. More often than not, you will receive impressions that make little or no sense to you whatsoever. Remember that they are not intended to make sense to you, only to their loved ones who will recognize and validate them.

Example: Souls may bring up jokes they shared with loved ones, personal moments or issues, triumphs or tragedies, important events or places, or meaningful material items such as jewelry or photos or keepsakes. Mostly this information is given as a validation of their presence and continued life. It is often accompanied by feelings or gestures of love, with the notion that they want their loved ones to know that they are still with them, even though their bodies are no longer.

Mediumship and Our Own Loved Ones

If there is one facet of mediumship that seems to possess the cruelest of ironies, it is that while we may have great success connecting with the departed loved ones of others, we may find it next to impossible to consciously connect with our own loved ones in spirit. Few things are so excruciatingly frustrating as finding ourselves drowning amidst the din of heavenly chatter, only to find it silent when it comes to the matters of our own heart. How is it possible to experience strangers with such clarity, while our nearest and dearest are so easily lost in the esoteric nebulousness?

There are many answers to that question, and many different reasons it may be difficult to connect with the ones we love. The most obvious reason is just that: we love them so much. As we know, emotion creates the psychic static that so often stands between us and them. They are with us, yet we do not perceive them consciously, despite their best efforts to reach us. Very often they reach us when we are off our guard, when our emotions are diverted. This is when they will slip in a thought, or a feeling, or a sign for us. Or they will come to us at night, in our sleep or semi-lucidity, when our conscious thoughts and feelings are no longer a barrier to our experience. These types of experiences should not be disregarded as figments of our imagination, or as "mere dreams," but instead investigated and considered as a potential genuine act of communication.

For many of us, there will come a time when we are able to consciously center ourselves and let go of our emotional attachments enough to experience those we love from the other side. We may sense their presence from time to time; we may find ourselves carrying on conversations with them, or feeling emotion from them. Unless we are deeply advanced and gifted psychics, the difficulty that arises at this point is validation. As we experience our loved ones abstractly through our psychic senses, we may be tempted to convince ourselves that our interactions are projections of our own wishful thinking or imagination. To the rational person, this is always a possibility.

When we connect with the loved ones of others, we usually get specific information as we go along that reaffirms the integrity of the process. Not only are we feeling that we are truly working with a specific soul, but we are also getting evidence to support that feeling. It is more difficult to get that evidence when working with the ones we love, because if we know them well, we already will know most of the evidence. We then have only the feeling to guide us. To many critical minds, this may not be enough.

If this becomes an issue in your personal work as a medium, consider some of the following suggestions.

Ask Your Loved One for a Validation

When you feel that you are connecting with your loved one, ask for a confirmation in the form of information that you are not privy to, but that can be validated by another friend or family member. Whatever information you receive, pass it around among your relatives to find out if it has any meaning. If you place it, you will find renewed inner confidence in your ability to connect with your loved one, and can rest assured that your experiences are more than indulgences of the heart.

Examples: This could be anything at all, from a vacation spot to a piece of jewelry, a nickname, or even a childhood pet.

Create a Personal Symbol

Once you have established that you are connecting with a certain soul, or even a guide, in the spiritual realm, ask to establish a certain symbol or impression to let you know that he or she is there with you. Depending on your sensibilities, this could be a visual symbol, a auditory sound or word, a feeling or sensation on a particular part of your body, or even a noise in the house.

To do this, simply ask, during a meditation, that the soul offer a means of identification for this purpose, and see what happens. It may be difficult at first, but with time and repetition, you may notice what recurs. Most often, souls will identify themselves immediately when they connect with us, so look for the very first impression as a probable starting point. Some souls will do this even without us asking. Others may not be inclined to do it at all. Nonetheless, this process can be a valuable guide as we function in our personal mediumship capacity.

Example: If your loved one was a doctor, you may get a brief visual impression of a stethoscope or a caduceus when the person is present. If she was an artist, you may ask for an impression of one of her paintings when she is coming through. This sort of identification can be helpful, allowing us always to be conscious of whom we are connecting with.

Frequently Asked Questions

Question: "How long after 'death' can a soul make contact with us?"

Explanation: Souls can touch in with us at any time after their passing. There are no constraints of time and space in the spiritual realm. Nonetheless, many souls reach out to us immediately after their physical death, and often try to comfort us with their energy when we are grieving for them. The issue of whether or not it is time to connect with a loved one depends more on the bereaved than on the soul who has crossed over. It may be better for us to have a certain degree of acceptance before connecting with our lost loved ones so that we may learn and grow from the experience in a healthy way.

Solution: Use your judgment as to whether or not the emotional environment is suitable for a mediumship session. If an individual is recently or severely bereaved, the experience may be difficult to process in a balanced manner. While we never want to deny anyone an opportunity to connect with a loved one, we do want to use good judgment regarding the appropriate time for that to happen.

Question: "The idea of mediumship scares me. Is the process frightening? Could spirits inhabit my body?"

Explanation: There is no reason to be afraid of mediumship. The actual process is usually a lot less dramatic than we are conditioned to expect. The process is generally a subtle, controlled one. Never do you lose or give up control of your consciousness, or of your body. When you work as a medium, you are training yourself to *notice* those in spirit; you do not need to alter your consciousness, nor does anything "spooky" happen. You simply learn to notice and communicate what you previously overlooked, or did not understand how to see.

Solution: Remember that mediumship is a natural process, not something to be feared.

Question: "What if souls tell us things we don't want to hear, or give us bad news about our future?"

Explanation: Most often the reason souls communicate with us is just to let us know that they are all right and are still with us, just in a different way. Souls are generally not interested in getting too tangled up in our worldly affairs. They simply want the best for us, and want us to know that they still share in our happiness.

Solution: Souls generally will not convey disturbing information during the mediumship process. However, if you do get any impressions that concern you, you can choose not to accept them or to share them with your sitter.

Question: "How do I know I am really connecting with a loved one and that I am not just picking up on telepathic thoughts from the physical world that describe memories of a soul in spirit?"

Explanation: It may be tempting at times to doubt that you are actually interacting with a live soul. You may wonder if you aren't picking up on some kind of remnant memories or mental energy from a person's loved ones. This is the reason souls often choose to bring through random and often previously unknown information to their loved ones. If the family or loved ones that you share psychic information with had no familiarity with the information coming through prior to the session, they have that much more validation of the integrity of the process.

It will not take you long to realize that souls come through with distinct personalities and are often very animated, much as they were in their physical lives. There is no doubt that an "interaction" is taking place, as the process feels very much like interacting with another human being.

Solution: Make a point to notice the individual and personal nature of the souls with whom you touch in. Notice how human they feel, as well as how spiritual they feel.

Question: "Is my pet still alive in the spiritual world?"

Explanation: Interestingly enough, this is one of the most common questions people ask when they approach mediumship. Animal souls, like human souls, do live on after death. Some mediums may pick up on pets during the process, and can often pick up on their names or physical descriptions.

Solution: Don't be surprised to hear a dog barking or to feel any kind of animal around you during the reading. When this happens, pass it on. Pets are a great source of validation, and people often are pleased to know that they are still around, too.

Summary

Mediumship offers us some of the most profound and life-changing perspectives on our world. It is a spiritual process that enables us to add a new dimension to our beliefs. Not only do we believe in the afterlife, we experience it. It is suddenly not so far away. Life becomes a more comfortable place in which we exist within a network of support, a network that is understood through both experience and faith.

Visions come not to polluted eyes.

—Mary Howitt

CHAPTER 20

REVELATION: *The Mystical Experience*

There will come a day for some of us when Heaven reveals itself to us through extraordinary means. We may have visions. We may see, hear, or touch beings of a nonphysical nature. We may have profound epiphanies that change our perspective of the world. As our souls experience higher levels of awareness, it is natural to be given insights into our true natures and the realities that transcend our perception.

Mystical experience is not an end in itself. Ideally, it is a by-product of our spiritual growth. Our minds and our perceptions naturally expand as we elevate our souls. Each of us will progress on our own path, with our own unique experiences. There is no specific guide or system to spirit revelation. Heaven will speak to us however we will best understand at a given time.

Though our soul's evolution contributes to our propensity for transcendental experience, it does not follow that all people who have mystical experiences or abilities are spiritually evolved. Not all spiritual people are psychic, and not all psychic people are spiritual. Some people are born with a natural openness to the spiritual realm, but their understanding needs time to catch up with it. There are others who, unfortunately, attempt to develop their intuition or even "psychic powers" without a genuine spiritual commitment. Either way, it is dangerous to embrace our inner power without education, awareness, and dedication to our higher purpose.

Our good intentions can easily be distorted if our goals or ideals are in the wrong place. Where is the wrong place? It is anywhere that isn't centered on our soul's growth and enlightenment. The wrong place can be ourselves, our egos, our possessions, our lovers, our duties, our status, our success, our responsibility, or our recreation. A person cannot serve two masters. Anything that becomes an end in itself and eclipses our dedication to Heaven threatens to distort our intuition, as well as our spiritual health in general. We must wholeheartedly accept divine will, and the hierarchy of our spiritual needs. This hierarchy is easily expressed:

- Love of God
- Love of our self
- Love of others

The heavenly spirit flows from God into us and out through the world, as we share our love and creativity with others. Similarly, love that we receive from others flows into our souls and back to our divine source. The flux of giving and receiving love encourages the evolution of our souls, and frees us from our worldly vices. Nevertheless, many of us fall into the trap of mistaking worldly ends for divine ends. Many of us center our will around ourselves or others, instead of around the higher good.

For example, it is natural for anyone who has lost a loved one to want to know that his or her loved one is still alive in spirit, and that they will be reunited someday. If we embrace our spirituality in order to gain insight into the continuous structure of life and to understand how we can improve our souls with the assistance and comfort of our loved ones in spirit, then our intent and purpose is genuine. On the other hand, if we embrace our spirituality for the sole purpose of reuniting with our lost loves, in order to gratify our dependent emotional needs, then our intent and purpose is distorted. In this latter instance, we are driven by a self-serving passion. Whether we realize it or not, our happiness is not contingent on anything other than being right with ourselves and God. When we chase after the things we think that we want and need, our lives can easily begin to revolve around a destructive center.

Any time we pursue spiritual ends with any intention other than evolving our souls selflessly into the divine presence, we run the risk of abusing our abilities. How can we serve ourselves and others with integrity if our intentions are in service to something other than the divine will? With the trust and faith that we are always safe in Heaven's hands, we open ourselves to truth in our own lives, as well as in the lives of those we touch.

Life after the Mystical Experience

Wonderful things happen when we release our fears and begin to take responsibility for our lives. Our burden is lighter. Our spirits are uplifted. We feel free. The psychic and physiological impact of such decision-making is more profound than most of us imagine. Not only can we heal ourselves, but we can alter our body chemistry and vibrational level to the point that we may be able to feel or perceive things that once were imperceptible to us. We may begin physically to see, hear, or feel the spiritual beings that exist around us. We may have extraordinary dreams or visions. The possibilities of spirit revelation are endless.

When the Heavens reveal to us directly, we are likely to be

surprised by how different the experience is from our preconceptions. There is, perhaps, no way to fully describe the indescribable. Many aspects of the spiritual realm are comparable to nothing we have known in our lives. Our experiences may seem so unprecedented that we may question the stability of our mental health. We may be challenged to integrate spiritual realities that surpass our previous religious or philosophical education. If this is the case, we should consider discussing our experiences with a minister or spiritual professional.

We should strive to understand the spiritual strides we have made in our lives that might have served as a catalyst for any deeply mystical experience. That is where the true information lies. Each experience is a message for us about ourselves. The experience itself may even have little meaning, aside from helping us to recognize that we currently are in a particularly meaningful part of our lives. It is often just beyond our darkest hours that we find spiritual illumination, for our own inner conquest opens us to the light.

Putting the Normal in Paranormal

One of the most important things we must remember when (or if) the spiritual realm manifests itself directly to our five physical senses is that, in most cases, this is a normal part of living a spiritual life. Because spiritual experience is so intangible, so nebulous in its very nature, the general public has little access to genuine metaphysical documentation, aside from the Bible.

If we cannot understand the reasons for our experiences, we are in danger of misinterpreting their meaning in our lives. If we are naive, we might be inclined to make the assumption that we were chosen to experience these phenomena because we are somehow more special or deserving than other people. On the other hand, if we are skeptics, we may soon find ourselves questioning our sanity. This leads us to the two most common misconceptions that are derived from mystical experience.

The Messiah Complex

Chances are, despite the fact that we may have been blessed with extraordinary and rare gifts of the spirit, we probably are not destined to "save" the world. Not exactly, anyway. Our immediate reaction to any profound supernatural events is often to think that we must be really special to deserve such a gift, that we must have some unique potential which God is leading us to. While in many ways this may be true, we must be careful not to overindulge our egos when situations like these occur. The truth is that you *are* special—but so is everyone else. We all are precious in God's eyes. Each one of us is as precious as the one lost sheep. The feeling of "uniqueness," of being the object of a special divine love, should not be misdirected to our egos. It is the supreme divine paradox that God loves each one of us as though each is the most precious soul of all.

Every one of us has a unique life mission. We all are here to bring God's goodness into the world. Heaven may reveal to us to inspire or affirm this process, or to assist us in our spiritual growth. Spiritual gifts can be the greatest affirmations of our religious beliefs and our metaphysical philosophies. When they are given to us, they are given not as rewards, and rarely as proof. Mostly they are given as signposts, to show us the way and to help us humbly help ourselves.

Denial

There are many people who are in no danger of developing a messiah complex after a spiritual experience, because they do not accept that they have had a spiritual experience at all. If they are lucky, they will have had a one-time experience, so that they can tuck it away and forget it ever happened. Denial is a very common reaction to the first-time supernatural experience. We say to ourselves, *That's impossible. I must've been dreaming, or surely I was hallucinating.* And that's usually enough to justify it and forget it.

But sometimes the spirit world persists. Heaven is not going to let us off so easy. How long can we deny it? How many times do we have to see the unseeable, or hear the unhearable, or feel the unfeelable before we are forced to reconcile it with reality? Before we get to the point at which we can actually answer that question, we usually question our sanity. And, of course, we are reluctant to seek advice on the matter because, surely, everyone else will question our sanity as well.

But, most of the time, we are not losing our minds. Most of the time, the spirit world is only challenging the boundaries of our minds. Perhaps it is time for us to expand our horizons. Perhaps it is time for us to educate ourselves, to understand the gifts we have been given. Before we resign ourselves to a self-diagnosis of madness, we should investigate all of the possibilities. The world is full of teachers and books and guidance that can lead us to a balanced acceptance of spiritual phenomena.

Most of us will pass through at least one of these two phases at some point in our spiritual development. Given time, we will learn to process our experience in a balanced way, and to integrate it into our lives.

Finally, we should always keep in mind that we do not experience the mystical by searching for it. We experience it by living. We can pray for a sign for as many hours as the day is long, and receive nothing. But that one right choice we make in our lives—that moment we decide to change, that moment we rise above ourselves—may alter us forever. For it is our decisions, and our actions, more than our intentions, that sow the seed of genuine spiritual growth.

Nearly all men can stand adversity, but if you want to test a man's character, give him power.

—Abraham Lincoln

CHAPTER 21

BEING A SENSITIVE SENSITIVE: *Free Will and Ethical Responsibility for Our Gifts*

We have a responsibility for our wisdom. With every new talent or ability comes power, and power must not be used carelessly. Spiritual awareness provides hope when all hope is lost. It gives direction where the path is overgrown. Any of us can become a bearer of light. We can be a source of guidance, inspiration, and strength, if we live and share in the spirit of God's peace.

Misuse, Abuse, and Fear of Psychic Power

Any power, including psychic power, can be misused and abused. Of course, we should approach all of our spiritual endeavors with the utmost level of integrity. Our personal ego or success must never take precedence over the truth.

At the other end of the scale are those who are reluctant to share their gifts with others. Initially, we may be somewhat uncomfortable in our roles as teachers, or healers, or spiritual advisers. It is not uncommon to have a fear of our responsibility, a fear that our intuition may guide us, or someone else, in the wrong direction. But if we are true to ourselves and responsible with our actions, this should not happen. If we are passing on genuinely inspired messages in an ethical manner, the worst we can do is pass on the *wrong* information. Though the information may be wrong, it would never be *bad*, because we only share information in the spirit of love and soul growth.

Prescribing Direct Courses of Action

Probably the most dangerous thing we can do when sharing our intuitive insights with others is to tell them what they "should" or "should not" do. We can use our intuition to advise, to guide, and to help people understand the potential outcome of their choices, but we can never take away their free will to choose. We can provide them with as much information as Heaven will give us, in order to help them see the true nature of their issues and to be able to make the best decisions in their lives. That is the best we can do. We can give people the understanding and the awareness that fuel their ability to respond positively to change and self-evolution. We cannot make things happen or force people to change.

Free Will and the Future

When we are receiving intuitive impressions, we may find ourselves learning information about the past, the present, or the future. Should we happen to be given information regarding future events, we must understand that we are not being given a 100 percent guarantee. We are being given the probabilities and potentials, based on the current course of action. Free will is never denied.

For example, if we receive an impression about a couple's future breakup, we should not necessarily interpret this to mean that this couple is doomed. We should stress that, if both parties continue on the track that they are now on in the relationship, there is a strong possibility that it will come to an end. But it is never too late to turn around. It is never too late to change our choices.

For this reason, no person can predict the future with absolute certainty. No psychic reading will be exempt from a margin of error. Intuition is always subject to change. We should, therefore, approach all intuitive information as signposts and guidance. We should not make the mistake of looking to our intuitive powers for easy answers or comforting outcomes.

• • •

When we embrace our intuition, we embrace a new way of living. We choose life, both temporal and eternal. We begin to live and work within the flux of transience and endlessness, ideally living fully aware in each moment that falls between. Life becomes more than a sequential series of events that start with the cradle and end with the grave; it becomes a meaningful interplay of past choices and future manifestations. We understand our free will and the vast potential that it offers us. We understand that we always have the power to change our lives.

The intuitive process is an adventure. There are new discoveries around every corner. With each passing day, there are more lights in the dark night. If we use our intuition in service to Heaven and with integrity and wisdom, we are capable of sharing an immense light with those we come in contact with. We also will nurture our own soul in the process. The more we illuminate others, the more we illuminate ourselves.

Your success is measured not by the achievement of your goal, but by being better this day than you were the last.

—Anonymous

Conclusion

All mastery takes time. Patience and dedication are the foundation of all talent, so we must be willing to work for what we love. Intuitive awareness is no exception. We should not be discouraged if our progress is slow, or if our abilities unfold in unique ways. We may have experiences or talents unlike those of any other person on earth. That is the beauty of having a personal relationship with the Eternal One. Heaven works with us all, reveals to us all, in our own special way.

There is no right or wrong way to experience God. We open our arms to Heaven and accept what we are given. Heaven will use us as instruments of its "way," based on our own individual strengths and talents. Each of us has his or her own path, own choices, and own destiny. As we co-create our lives with God, we understand which parts of our destiny come to us, and which parts we are capable of manifesting ourselves. Together, with Heaven, we create our life.

Intuition allows this co-creation to manifest serendipitously, as our will and the Divine will become one. As our intuition becomes clearer, the purpose and higher meaning of our life situations also become clearer. We are able to use our higher awareness to assist ourselves, and others, in the process of self-evolution, which is the evolution of the soul toward perfection. This is the true spirit of all psychic work—to bring awareness, understanding, and union with the heavenly spirit.

Each of us will be called to use our intuition in a different way. Some may be called to ministry, while others may be called to counseling or teaching. Many of us will remain as silent helpers and healers, offering guidance and support without reward. Whether or not we choose to use our talents to serve others, our own personal lives will always be enriched by our intuitive awareness. What better way to help others than by helping ourselves?

The journey within is one filled with unexpected mystery, adventure, discovery, joy, and amazement. There is more life inside us, and in the invisible space around us, than we could imagine in our wildest dreams. In truth, life exceeds imagination. When we understand that the spiritual realm is vast, alive, and opulent beyond our conception, the world becomes a very interesting place.

It is time for many of us to explore the greatest frontier, the uncharted territory that lies beyond time and beyond space—the strange and beautiful landscape of our soul and our heavenly home. An eternity of wisdom and life lies waiting for discovery by those who are willing to embark on the mystical adventure. All of our resources are within us. All we need is our heart, our mind, and the will to be something better than we are.

About the Author

Kim Chestney is a certified intuitive counselor, astrologer, and Reiki Master. Educated in the United States, England, and Canada, she is a professional artist and writer, and is the founder of mysticstudio, inc. in Pittsburgh, Pennsylvania. Kim has been extensively trained in metaphysical principles, healing, meditation, yoga, classical ballet, and meditative movement. Kim can be contacted via her Web site at *www.kimchestney.com*.

INDEX